THE
NORMAN KINGS

THE NORMAN KINGS

James Chambers

Introduction by Antonia Fraser

Weidenfeld and Nicolson
London

Series designed by
Paul Watkins
Layout by Sheila Sherwen
Picture research by
Caroline Lucas

Filmset by Keyspools Ltd.
Golborne, Lancs.
Printed and bound in Great Britain
by Morrison & Gibb Ltd,
London and Edinburgh

Contents

Introduction

In a mere eighty-eight years the Norman Kings of England transformed our country from a long-beleaguered island into an unassailable fortress. Stone castles, symbols of Norman dominance (many of which still stand today) replaced the wooden structures of the Anglo-Saxons. The power of the Norman church is still commemorated by the great cathedrals of that era, including the austere grandeur of Winchester, the lofty beauty of Durham and the more ornate splendour of Peterborough. In addition, this was a period which saw the evolution of the first governmental institutions of the modern state – notably the Curia Regis, from which ultimately a parliamentary assembly would derive – and a monarchy whose strength was only rivalled by that of the Normans in Sicily. At the same time, valuable types of immigrants, Flemish weavers and Jews to supply the king's financial needs, helped to lay the foundations of what James Chambers describes as the 'burgeoning bourgeois capitalism of England'.

The kings who presided over this remarkable period of enterprise and change were not however in themselves figures of nobility, let alone chivalry. William the Conqueror, a brutal man of enormous size, captured England against what seemed impossible odds as much by ruthless will as by good luck and the weakness of his enemies. William Rufus suffered from the combined defects of evil temper, unattractive appearance and a stammer, and his circle of debauched and sycophantic courtiers did nothing to contribute to an image of gallantry.

Even the most distinguished of their number, Henry I, the 'Lion of Justice', to whose reformation of English law and government so much is owed, was animated more strongly by a desire for a great Anglo-French empire than by any particular philanthropy towards his English subjects. When the news came that his only legitimate son William the Atheling had been drowned in the *White Ship*, it was the collapse of that dream of empire which rendered him distraught, rather than the prospect of civil disorder which might follow a dispute over the succession. Indeed, the anarchic conflicts of his nephew Stephen and his daughter Matilda after his death originated at least in part in Henry I's wilful imposition of his daughter upon the Curia Regis as his successor.

Yet, for all their faults, and for all the repressive intentions of many of their policies, the Norman kings altered our society permanently and fundamentally for the better. James Chambers pursues this interesting dichotomy between the nature of the monarchs concerned and the effects of their régime in a fascinating and highly readable study. The nineteenth-century historians were wont to mourn the departure of the Anglo-Saxon civilization after the fatal defeat of Harold at Hastings: nevertheless this civilization was itself already in decay. The Normans brought energy, essential organization, and a vigorous Latin (and French) culture into what had been a declining Teutonic world.

Antonia Fraser

Acknowledgements

Photographs and illustrations were supplied or are reproduced by kind permission of the following (numbers in italics indicate colour illustrations):

J. Allan Cash 194; Bibliothèque Municipale, Dijon 210 top; Bibliothèque Municipale, Rouen 28; Bibliothèque Nationale, Paris 74, 152 (photo Roger-Viollet), 156–7; Bibliothèque de la Ville d'Avranches 26; Bodleian Library, Oxford 63, 68 top, 76, 100, *114*, *115*, 142, 160, 200–1, 211 top; British Library 50, 53, 69 centre and top, *71*, 88–9, 98, *118–19*, *122*, 129, 138–9, 155, *162*, *171*, 198, 206; British Museum *10–11*, 16, 17, 20, 21, 22–3, 56, 57, *70*, 82, 96 bottom, 113, 120–1, 126–7, 131, 161, 168–9, 176, 179, 181; William Burrell Collection, Glasgow 44; The syndics of Cambridge University Library 33, 36–7, 43; Chèze-Brown 54–5, 61, 102–3, 103, 146–7; The Master and Fellows of Corpus Christi College Cambridge 13, 48, 172; Dean and Chapter of Durham Cathedral 105, endpapers; Department of the Environment (Crown Copyright) 182–3, 195; His Grace the Duke of Roxburghe 178; e.t. archive 141; Giraudon *78–9*, 150; Glasgow University Library *3*, 92–3, 96 top; Michael Holford *2*, *14–15*, 97 top left and bottom, 135, *174*, *175*, 204; Angelo Hornak 134 right; Houghton Library, Harvard University 64–5; A. F. Kersting 95, 101, 124, 182, 191, 205, 209; Leonard von Matt, Switzerland (photo Buochs) 97 top right; Musée des Antiquités, Rouen (photo Ellebé) 187; National Monuments Record (Crown Copyright) 73, 188; Phaidon Picture Archive 32, 35, 40–1, 46, 49 bottom, 68–9 bottom; Photo Boudot-Lamotte, Paris 164; Popperfoto 186; Public Record Office 80–1, 84–5, 108, 143, 144, 213; Roger-Viollet 31, 90, 106–7; Edwin Smith 134 left; The Master and Fellows of Trinity College, Cambridge (Mansell Collection) 210 bottom; Victoria and Albert Museum 207, 211 bottom; Weidenfeld and Nicolson archive 72, 77, 190.

Picture research by Caroline Lucas
Maps and family trees by John Gilkes

1 England
and
Normandy

IN THE GREY twilight of 14 October 1066 a small group of leaderless Saxon housecarls, many of them wounded and all of them wearied by a long day of battle, scrambled through a deep ditch between Senlac hill and the woods that straddled the road from Hastings to London. At the top of the far bank they rallied, and when the detachment of Norman knights that had been hard behind them began to wheel away, it looked as though the ditch, darkness and defiance of a defeated enemy had deterred the victors from a needless and wasteful pursuit. But as the Normans rode back up the corpse-strewn hill, where the body of the English king lay naked and mutilated beyond the brow, the huge figure of their duke was seen riding down to meet them; and after he had been among them for a moment, they turned again, advancing to the attack. As night fell the remnants of the last professional corps of royal Saxon bodyguards died to a man, and an era in England ended.

Only fifty years had passed since England had last been conquered. It had been a conquest that wrought little change in the lives of the thegns and freemen who were to fight at Hastings, but it had deposed their Saxon dynasty and in so doing it had sown the seeds of the rivalry and discord that were to expose their kingdom to its final subjugation in 1066.

In April 1016, while England was crumbling under the impact of a Danish invasion, the Saxon king, Ethelred the Unready, died. After they had fought to a standstill, his gallant son Edmund Ironside and King Cnut of Denmark agreed to divide the kingdom between them. But at the end of November in the same year Edmund also died, and when the Saxon king's council – known as the Witan – assembled in accordance with its right to elect a successor, there was no Saxon candidate in the exhausted and despondent kingdom who could be expected to withstand the Danes. Edmund Ironside's sons, Edmund and Edward, were in their cradles; his brother Eadwig, who was the only surviving son of Ethelred's marriage to a Saxon, was only eighteen years old, inexperienced and ill-supported; and Alfred and Edward, the sons of Ethelred's second marriage to the Duke of Normandy's sister Emma, were boys of only thirteen and twelve. Accepting the inevitable, the Witan elected Cnut as king of all England.

Within a year, Cnut had neutralized the potential challengers

12

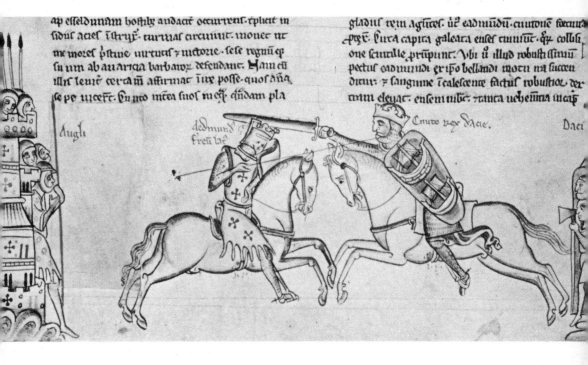

to his throne. Eadwig, who attempted a rebellion, was captured and executed; and Edmund Ironside's sons were sent to be fostered by King Olaf of Sweden, who, instead of disposing of them as had been hinted, sent them to safety in Hungary, where King Stephen brought them up as princes. The threat of Ethelred's half-Norman sons was removed by their own mother. To her discredit, Emma accepted Cnut's offer of marriage on condition that he recognized any son that she might bear him as his heir. When he agreed she abandoned Alfred and Edward to the fortunately tender care of their uncle, Duke Richard II, in Normandy.

Cnut left England as he had found it. From the outset he appointed Saxons to the highest offices in the Church and State, and, since he rewarded his soldiers with money rather than land, he allowed most of the Saxon landlords to retain their estates. During his reign, England became part of a Scandinavian empire that included Denmark, Norway and the Hebrides, London rose to be the centre of trade for northern Europe, and in peaceful prosperity the Saxons learned to accept and then to welcome his government.

The Danegeld, an English war tax which Ethelred had

Single combat between Edmund Ironside and Cnut at Deerhurst, where they divided the kingdom of England in 1016, from the thirteenth-century *Chronica Majora* by Matthew Paris.

OVERLEAF Harold landing on the Norman coast, from the Bayeux Tapestry.

HAROLD: H

A Saxon sword, which was forged on the pattern of the Viking swords.

sometimes used to buy off Viking raiders, continued to be levied for the defence of the realm, and with this Cnut supported a fleet and a small standing army of housecarls, who were probably the finest infantry in Europe. Like the first dragoons of a later age, the housecarls rode to battle and then dismounted to fight on foot. They wore conical helmets and knee-length coats of mail, known as byrnies. They carried long, tapering shields, javelins and Viking swords, and their principal weapons were their huge, gold-encrusted battle-axes, which they swung two-handed with such force that it was said they could fell a horse and its rider with a single blow. At first they were all Danes, but Saxons were soon accepted into their ranks, and after a while their corps was predominantly English. Although some of them owned land, they were not bound to the king by any feudal obligation; they were professional soldiers who simply served him in return for their eight marks per annum. They had their own code of honour and their own guild, to which the king belonged.

In tradition and life-style the housecarls were closer to their contemporaries in Japan, the first samurai, than they were to the landed knights and barons who formed the élite corps in the armies of feudal Europe. In peace they formed the king's bodyguard and in battle they fought around him, supported by the fyrd — the English militia — in which every thegn and freeman was bound to serve.

The thegns, who were the barons of England, lived on estates that varied in size from single villages to huge earldoms which embraced several shires. In the Anglo-Danish kingdom it was a rule of law that 'every man must have a lord', and a chain of allegiance that had grown out of tribal loyalties ran from the king through the earls and lesser thegns to the serfs who laboured in the fields and workshops. In the south and west of England, which the Danes had hardly penetrated, the thegns enjoyed primitive but plentiful ease in their richly carved and painted wooden halls, while the serfs gave them labour and a share of their produce in return for protection and justice. On those estates that belonged to the Church, the serfs as often as not served bishops who lived in halls with women in a style that was no different to the thegns'. There was, however, greater freedom in the north-eastern area, known as the Danelaw,

An eleventh-century Saxon battle scene.

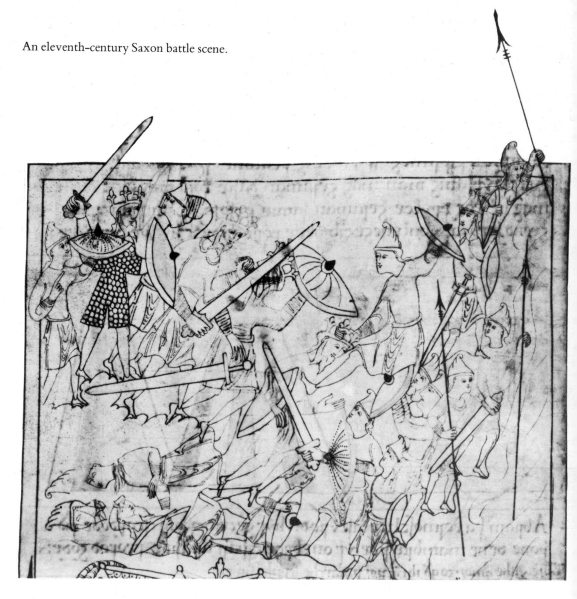

where Saxons had been driven out by a long series of Danish raiders, and where the land was tilled by as many small freeholders as serfs.

Like Cnut's empire, which he ruled through viceroys, England was effectively governed by the earls, over whom the kings had no more control than their rights to revenues and military service. Even the administration of justice had been delegated by Cnut's Saxon predecessors, who had given thegns and prelates the right to hold their own private courts. The king's courts of the shires and the smaller hundreds, into which

17

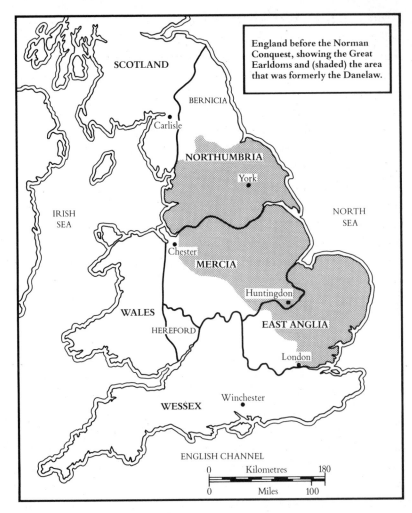

England before the Norman Conquest, showing the Great Earldoms and (shaded) the area that was formerly the Danelaw.

the shires were divided, remained, and the shire reeves, or sheriffs, who were technically the king's representatives, still presided over the shire courts with the local earls and bishops. However, the majority of these courts had fallen under the control of the larger landowners and, although legislation had created some common law, most of the law which the royal and private courts administered had evolved out of local customs and varied from shire to shire. With the virtual independence of its jealous earls, its differing degrees of freedom and the disparity of its laws, customs and races, the kingdom of England was united in little but name.

During Cnut's reign, the earl who rose to the greatest prominence was his Saxon favourite, Godwin, whom he had created Earl of Wessex. When Cnut died in 1035, Godwin began to play the part of a cynical, self-seeking king-maker. At first he joined Queen Emma in supporting her son, Harthacnut, against Cnut's popular half-Saxon bastard Harold Harefoot, who had been elected by the Witan. When the issue was complicated by the arrival of Emma's elder son, Alfred, who came over from Normandy to press his claim as heir to Ethelred, Godwin welcomed him and then handed him over to Harold, who had him blinded before he was butchered. But when Harthacnut delayed in Denmark, Godwin switched his allegiance to the grateful Harold until, on Harold's sudden, childless death in 1040, the Witan wisely elected Harthacnut – who was preparing an invasion anyway – and Godwin hurriedly negotiated a pardon for his brief disloyalty. Harthacnut brought his mother and his half-brother Edward to live with him at court, but it was the only decent deed of his mercifully short reign. By the time he died less than two years later, the Saxons had lost their love for Danish kings.

Cnut had left no other sons, and the most obvious candidate for the English throne was Emma's last son Edward, who was also the only surviving son of King Ethelred. Edmund Ironside's sons were forgotten in Hungary, and although some Danish earls supported Cnut's nephew Swein, Godwin bribed them to abandon him. When the Witan eagerly restored the Saxon dynasty by electing the pious and unworldly Edward, who was to be remembered as Edward the Confessor, Godwin had at last found a king whom he thought he might be able to dominate. Edward granted estates to members of Godwin's family, including the earldom of East Anglia to his son Harold, and, in spite of the fact that according to some chroniclers he had taken a vow of chastity, he agreed to marry Godwin's daughter Edith. Yet the generous, docile new king can hardly have trusted the man who betrayed his brother Alfred. As time passed, the influence of other earls increased, the childless royal marriage thwarted Godwin's ambition to be the grandfather of a king, and Godwin began to suspect the Norman sympathies of a king who was half-Norman by birth and entirely Norman by education.

Like the Danelaw of England, the duchy of Normandy, in which Edward the Confessor spent his youth and early

King Edward the
Confessor, who was
educated in Normandy
and introduced Norman
commanders and prelates
into England, from a
fourteenth-century
manuscript.

childhood, had grown out of a Viking settlement. But under the influence of the surrounding Latin civilization it had developed into a vigorous, menacingly ambitious state that was very different to the factious and decadent Anglo-Danish kingdom that Edward was to inherit. During the ninth century, soon after the first Vikings began to land on the shores of north-eastern England, others sailed up the river Seine in France and settled around its lower banks. In 911, under the Treaty of Saint-Clair-sur-Epte, the French king, Charles the Simple, accepting that he could no longer recover his coastal domains from the northmen, ceded them to their leader, Rollo. The northmen continued to expand their territory, and by the time Queen Emma's father, Richard I, assumed the title of duke, Normandy had become as powerful and independent as Flanders, Anjou, Aquitaine, Burgundy and the other sup-

King Edward the Confessor at a banquet, from a fourteenth-century manuscript.

21

A fifteenth-century representation of Rollo, the first count of Normandy, landing at Saint Martin's gate in Rouen, with the city of Jumièges in the background.

posedly defensive principalities with which the French kings had surrounded themselves. Within its boundaries the duke exercised all the prerogatives of a king, and so great were his wealth and the strength of his army that his allegiance to the king of France was only nominal.

Rollo's Vikings had been less numerous than the Vikings who landed in England, and there is no evidence to suggest that they were followed by successive waves of settlers. In the towns and along the coast they became merchants and fishermen, and throughout their conquered domains they replaced the slaughtered or expelled aristocracy. But the serfs who worked their land were the Franks who had been there before them, there were no Viking smallholders as there were on the farms of north-eastern England, and the language remained the language of the peasant majority. In England, the villages of Viking landlords like Grim and Thor were known by the totally Scandinavian names of Grimsby and Thoresby, but the villages of their kinsmen in Normandy were called Grimonville and Tourville.

From the outset the Norman rulers married into the families of their powerful neighbours. As well as their language, they adopted their culture and religion, and they studied and practised their methods of warfare. They spent more time and money than any other princes in the training and equipping of their army. Like the housecarls, their soldiers wore the Scandinavian helmets and coats of mail, which they called hauberks, but they abandoned the ponies and axes that they had brought with them in their longships, they bought strong, agile war-horses, known as destriers, from their neighbours and learned to fight from their saddles with swords and lances. As valued allies, they gained experience, prestige and wealth in the feudal wars of France until, by the middle of the eleventh century, the descendants of men who were masters of the sea and lightning raids had become the most formidable heavy cavalry in northern Europe.

As conquerors surrounded by potential enemies, the early rulers of Normandy had no need to impose feudal obligations in order to raise an army. Survival or greed were enough to make men fight; and to retain their estates, in which they had only been rewarded with a life interest, barons could be expected to remain loyal. But by the middle of the eleventh century, during the reign of William the Bastard, Norman society was beginning to develop symptoms of the territorial feudalism that prevailed in the rest of France: serfs were tied to the land, estates were becoming hereditary and, in return for their land, some barons, bishops and abbots were required to provide the duke with specific quotas of knights for up to forty days in each year.

French feudalism allowed for less freedom than the English social system, but it suffered from the same inherent weaknesses: the great principalities were as disruptive and defiantly independent as the English earldoms, and even within those principalities there were large estates whose lords were too powerful to be challenged. In Normandy, however, there were no such estates. The duke was by far the richest man in his duchy, and he had tighter control over his subjects and their economy than any other European prince. The estates of his barons were small; the wooden castles which dominated these estates from high, earthen mounds could not be built without a licence and had to be surrendered on demand; and within each county the courts, the army, the collection of revenues and the maintenance of order were under the control of viscounts, who were directly appointed by the duke.

By the middle of the eleventh century there were few, if any, Norman barons whose Viking blood had not been diluted by marriage, and there were many who had no Viking blood at all. The success of the Norman army had attracted soldiers of fortune from the rest of France and even Germany, who had remained to live on the estates with which the dukes had rewarded them. Similarly, since the beginning of that century, the generous endowment of new monasteries and ducal support for religious reforms had led to an influx of foreign prelates and scholars. In 1039 a teacher called Lanfranc arrived from Italy and a few years later established a famous school at the little monastery of Bec, where among his pupils he taught Anselm of Lucca, who was to become Pope in 1061, and another Anselm from Aosta, who was to surpass his teacher as one of the great theologians and philosophers of his age, and to follow him from Bec to the see of Canterbury.

In hardly more than a century, Norman society had lost all

Duke Robert the Devil, the father of the Conqueror, offering his gauntlet to Saint Michael, from a twelfth-century manuscript.

semblance of its Scandinavian origins. Among the Norman barons a little of the Vikings blood remained in their spirit of adventure and their pride in the prowess of their army. But when that blood brought them back to the sea and led them to conquer and settle in southern Italy, Sicily, Antioch and England, the language that they took with them was French, the culture, such as it was, was Franco-Italian, and the instinct for strong, centralized government was uniquely their own.

Queen Emma of England's brother, Richard II, was succeeded as duke of Normandy by his sons. The first, Richard III, died childless, and the second, Robert the Devil, who was betrothed to King Cnut's sister, died while returning from a pilgrimage to Jerusalem before the marriage could take place. Duke Robert did have a son, however – the result of a romantic, youthful liaison with a Falaise tanner's daughter called Herlève – and before setting out for Jerusalem he had persuaded the French king and the Norman barons to acknowledge the bastard William as his heir. William was no more than eight years old when his father died in 1035, the same year as King

26

Cnut, and for the next twenty-three years he was to be beleaguered by conspiracies, rebellions and invasions.

Under the protection of his feudal lord, King Henry I of France, and his aunt's stepson, Count Baldwin V of Flanders, who was also the French king's brother-in-law, William survived the murder of three guardians and the first twelve years of almost constant anarchy. In 1047, commanding his own army for the first time and supported by King Henry, he suppressed the last dangerous rebellion at the battle of Val-ès-Dunes. In the following year he joined Henry in a successful campaign against Count Geoffrey Martel of Anjou, who had invaded Maine. With these demonstrations of his military prowess and his capacity to control his own duchy, he became acceptable to Count Baldwin as a worthy husband for his daughter Matilda. But, for uncertain reasons of their own, Pope Leo IX forbade the marriage, which took place anyway, and King Henry, who was probably apprehensive, withdrew his support and made an alliance with his former enemy, Geoffrey Martel. Determined to recover Normandy and destroy its precocious duke, the armies of the new alliance invaded it in 1054 and again in 1058, only to be defeated and driven out each time at the battles of Mortemer and Varaville. By 1060, when both Henry and Geoffrey died, newly confident and victorious Normandy was no longer on the defensive. In 1062, while the Norman adventurers who had already conquered southern Italy were advancing through Sicily a thousand miles away, William conquered Maine on the pretext that its late count had bequeathed it to him; and in 1064 he marched west to impose his suzerainty on Brittany.

In keeping with his ambitions and his success, Duke William of Normandy was an awesome figure. He was stern, nearly six foot tall and heavily built, and his voice was harsh. Like his barons, he was illiterate, brutal and as fond of battle as of hunting. But by all accounts he was devout, and he was puritanical in his abhorrence of drunkenness, promiscuity and married priests. He was unfashionably faithful to his tiny, fragile wife Matilda; and it was said of him that he was abstemious with food and drink, although this hardly accords with the bulk of his body, which increased with the years. A supporter of religious reforms and a generous patron of the

Church, he formed his only deep and lasting friendship with Lanfranc, who was as much his opposite in taste and temperament as he was his equal in strength of character. Their one brief but violent quarrel arose when Lanfranc denounced William's forbidden marriage as a sin, but after their reconciliation it was due in part to Lanfranc's advocacy that Pope Nicholas II gave the marriage a dispensation in 1059. Yet the influence of Lanfranc never moderated William's restless and ruthless disposition, which had already been shaped and developed in the hard disenchanting school of his dangerous youth. It was there that his considerable military talent had been brought to an early maturity; it was there that he had been taught the value of patience and deceit; and it was there, while acquiring the basic skills of diplomacy, that he had learned how to lay the foundations of convincing claims to counties or kingdoms.

While Duke William was building his reputation in Europe, the Norman influence which Earl Godwin had feared was becoming evident in England. With a natural preference for French-speaking men, with whom he had more in common than his Saxon and Danish subjects, and with a need to have trustworthy supporters who would strengthen his hand against Godwin, Edward the Confessor was appointing Normans to some of the offices of Church and State.

Normans were given command of the vital ports along the south coast in Sussex. The earldom of Hereford was granted to a Norman called Ralph, who introduced Norman military methods in the defence of the Welsh marches and, to the indignation of the Saxon inhabitants, allowed his rapacious knights to build castles. Several vacant bishoprics were given to Normans; and, in March 1051, with the grudging consent of the Witan and against the ardent opposition of Earl Godwin, the Norman Robert of Jumièges was appointed Archbishop of Canterbury. But, if the story is true, the most ominous example of the king's Norman sympathies was unknown even to Earl Godwin. After his appointment, Robert of Jumièges left at once to receive his cloak of honour, known as a *pallium*, from Pope Leo IX. According to the history of Duke William which was written by Robert's fellow-monk, William of Jumièges, the new archbishop travelled via Normandy, where he delivered a

OPPOSITE An illumination from a Saxon missal which was presented to the abbey of Jumièges by its former abbot, Robert, who was appointed to the see of Canterbury by Edward the Confessor.

message in which the childless king of England promised to name the Norman duke as his heir.

During the summer, while Robert of Jumièges was still away, the relationship between King Edward and Earl Godwin deteriorated to the verge of civil war. Doubting the reliability of his own reticent fyrd, Godwin decided for the time being to flee with his family, and, in their absence, Edward declared them outlaws and confiscated their estates. But at the end of the year, according to the *Anglo-Saxon Chronicle*, Edward received a visit from his cousin Duke William, and it may have been this that led some Saxons to share Godwin's suspicions. When he and his son Harold returned the following spring at the head of an army, they were welcomed with such overwhelming enthusiasm that the king could do nothing but capitulate. Their estates and authority were returned to them, and several Norman courtiers and bishops were expelled, among them Archbishop Robert of Jumièges, who was replaced by Godwin's friend Stigand, Bishop of Winchester and former chaplain to King Cnut.

In pressing for the appointment of Archbishop Stigand, however, Godwin had unwittingly armed his Norman enemies with an influential ally. While Robert of Jumièges lived, the popes refused to recognise Stigand. It was not until 1258 that he was able to buy his *pallium* from the anti-Pope Benedict x. But within the year Benedict was ousted by the Burgundian Pope Nicholas ii, who was a friend of the Norman conquerors in southern Italy; and Nicholas's successor, who took the name Alexander ii and who was the incumbent at Rome when Edward the Confessor died in 1066, was Anselm of Lucca, a former pupil of Lanfranc. To these pro-Norman reformers, Stigand was not just a schismatic who owed his appointment to the anti-Pope, he was also a usurper who had replaced a Norman and he was, perhaps unjustly, the ungodly primate of a dissolute clergy.

Within months of his triumphant return Godwin choked to death at a dinner with the king. His earldom and his influence were inherited by his son Harold, who exploited them so effectively that, by 1057, he and his brothers held every earldom in England except Mercia. Harold allied himself to Mercia's Earl Edwin by marrying his sister Edith, but in 1065 he suffered

OPPOSITE The ruins of the abbey of Jumièges. Dedicated in 1067, it is one of the few, surviving, large, Norman churches to have been built before the conquest.

After landing in Normandy, Harold meets Duke William at his court, from the Bayeux Tapestry.

a setback when the people of Northumbria revolted against his brother Tostig and chose Edwin's brother Morcar as their earl in his place. Unable to negotiate Tostig's reinstatement, Harold made the best of it by acknowledging his brother-in-law, and the bitter Tostig went into exile to plan his vengeance.

In 1064 Harold visited Normandy, and while he was there he served with distinction in Duke William's army during his campaign in Brittany. The reason for the visit is uncertain: some chroniclers say that he was shipwrecked on a fishing expedition; others that he went to negotiate the release of some hostages; and the Norman chroniclers, who cannot be acquitted of bias, say that he went to affirm King Edward's promise that William would succeed him and to swear his own allegiance to the duke as well. Unless Harold was held prisoner, in which case he might have said anything to obtain his freedom, the Norman

story seems very unlikely. By then Edward must have realised that his Witan would prefer a Saxon successor: in 1054 he had invited Edmund Ironside's surviving son Edward the Exile to return from Hungary, which suggests that he might have supported this more suitable candidate if the exile had not died a few days after he landed in 1057. Assuming that he made a promise to William in the first place, he would hardly have sent his leading Saxon subject to confirm it. Above all, Harold would not have acknowledged William sincerely when he now had expectations of his own. He was by far the most powerful man in England and the only one capable of organizing a united defence against the invasion which was being prepared by King Harald Hardrada of Norway. Whoever the ailing Edward nominated, the Witan was likely to elect Harold; and whether it did or not, Harold could take the throne if he wanted it.

Harold crowning himself in Westminster Abbey, from the thirteenth-century *Estoire de Seint Aedward le Roi* by Matthew Paris.

33

It seems likely that Harold's succession had been agreed before Edward's death. Such was the speed of his election that it could hardly have been otherwise. Edward the Confessor died on 5 January 1066 and on his deathbed acknowledged Harold as his inevitable successor. At dawn on the next day he was buried in the new abbey at Westminster, which had only been consecrated eight days before. By the end of the morning Harold had been elected by the Witan and enthroned at High Mass in the abbey.

However, there were powerful men in Europe who saw themselves as the rightful successors to Edward, and there was one vengeful exile who was ready to help them. It may be that the speed of Harold's election was due to the certainty that he would soon be called upon to defend his kingdom. Cnut's nephew, King Swein of Denmark, claimed that the succession had been promised to him when Edward had been chosen in his place; King Harald Hardrada of Norway, whose army was already assembled, claimed that the childless Harthacnut had promised the throne to his predecessor, King Magnus; Duke William of Normandy claimed that Edward had promised it to him; and Harold's brother Tostig was raising his own army in Flanders to take what he could.

Since the English monarchy was elective, the promises of a previous king, or even royal blood, amounted at best to grounds for being considered as a candidate. By blood, the best candidate was the twelve-year-old Edgar the Atheling, the heir apparent, Edward's great-nephew and the grandson of Edmund Ironside, who had been brought to England by his father, Edward the Exile, in 1057. But, as its record shows, the Witan tended to elect the most powerful candidate within the kingdom, which in this case was Harold, and the fact that it had usually chosen men of royal blood before was due to the loyalty that such men commanded among the people, rather than any concept of divine right. If the chosen king turned out to be too weak to defend his throne, the Witan was ready to elect the victorious challenger. Whatever the principle, the election of the Witan was in fact no more than the traditional formality upon which unassailable candidates or successful challengers based their sovereignty. If anyone wanted to challenge the election in battle, there was no reason to suppose that the Witan

ODO·EPS· ROTBERT·:ISTE·II

WIL LELM·

would not elect them if they were successful, but there was no law, tradition or precedent upon which they could base their claim as a right. Once the Witan had elected Harold, Harold was the rightful king of England.

In Europe, however, where William had been promoting the justice of his cause, the niceties of English tradition were unknown, and Harold's case went unheard. Having dispatched a protest to England, William declared his intention to invade

OVERLEAF King Harald Hardrada of Norway landing in the Humber and defeating the northern fyrd at Fulford on 20 September, 1066, from *La Estoire de Seint Aedward.*

35

and sent a mission to seek the support of Rome. There were some in the Papal Curia who saw the invasion as unjustified, but the arguments of the great reforming Archdeacon Hildebrand and the Norman sympathies of Pope Alexander II prevailed. The rights and wrongs of the case were of little importance beside the opportunity to return England and its schismatic clergy to the fold of the Church of Rome. The pious duke could be relied upon to support religious reform and restore Robert of Jumièges to the see of Canterbury. Endorsing the invasion, the Pope blessed a banner and sent it to Normandy.

Papal approval enhanced William's propaganda and assured the acquiescence or indifference of other princes, many of whom hoped that the pretentious crusade might at least preoccupy the dangerous duke and might at best satisfy his ambition. But it was still necessary to leave a substantial army to defend Normandy during William's absence and, even if the Norman barons had been willing to fight abroad, the duchy did not have the manpower to provide a second army for the invasion of England. While his envoys bargained for mercenaries in the rest of France, William and a clique of enthusiastic magnates – which included his mother's legitimate sons Robert, Count of Mortain, and Odo, Bishop of Bayeux – coaxed the reticent barons in Normandy. With promises of land, money and even rich English brides, the barons were slowly won over. Throughout the spring, the Norman nucleus of William's army mustered, transports were assembled in the ports, new ships were built and soldiers of fortune arrived not only from the Norman dominions of Brittany and Maine but from Poitou, Anjou, Aquitaine, Flanders and even as far away as Aragon and the Norman colonies in southern Italy. A few of the French contingents were led by great feudal barons like Eustace of Boulogne, but the majority of the mercenaries were landless adventurers, who left little behind them and who, like the Normans, risked only their lives in return for a share of the spoils.

In England, meanwhile, Harold was preparing his defences. The fyrds were summoned, a fleet was mustered, and an enormous number of coins was minted to pay for them. On 24 April the appearance of Halley's comet was interpreted by Harold's superstitious subjects as an omen of disaster. Soon afterwards, at the beginning of May, while Harold was in York exhorting the commanders of the northern fyrd to face the Norwegians, the first invaders landed in the south under his brother Tostig. Tostig had apparently been negotiating with the Viking kings and the Norman duke, but his landing does not seem to have been part of any combined plan, and his army, which was mostly composed of pirates and Flemish mercenaries, was no match for a nation that had been mobilized on an unprecedented scale. When he heard that Harold was marching to meet him, Tostig sailed north with his sixty ships and landed in the Humber, where he was routed by Earl Edwin. He fled ingloriously to Scotland with his strength so reduced by casualties and desertion that he had only enough men to man twelve of his ships.

To the people of England, the impending invasion from Norway was a greater threat than an invasion from Normandy. King Harald Hardrada (the Ruthless) was the mightiest Viking warrior of his age. Until a treaty in 1064, he had regularly ravaged the north of Denmark, and as a young man he had led the Byzantine empress's Varangian guards to victory in Italy, Sicily, North Africa and the Holy Land. Yet Harold left the north to the northern earls and concentrated his own energies in the south. During July he assembled the Wessex fyrd along the coast and stationed himself with his fleet on the Isle of Wight, ready to intercept the invaders at sea. But the winds blew from the north and continued throughout August, confining the Norman ships to the safety of their coast, while Harold's supplies diminished and his ships became progressively less seaworthy through constantly patrolling in heavy weather. Eventually, on 8 September, when the wind had not changed and the summer seemed over, the last Saxon king of England dismissed the soldiers of his fyrd to bring in their battered harvests, ordered his fleet to the Thames for a refit, and returned to London with his housecarls.

ERFEC
TVS:EST

2 The Conques

ET FVGA: VI

of England

BEFORE THEY BLEW out of England onto the coast of Normandy, the northerly winds that kept Duke William's fleet at bay blew down from the pole past Norway; and over the North Sea, in the middle of September 1066, they filled the sails of 300 Viking longships.

King Harold had been in London for hardly more than a week when he learned that King Harald Hardrada, who had been joined by Tostig off the coast of Scotland, had landed in the Humber and was advancing on York. With his housecarls and a hurriedly assembled fyrd from the home counties, Harold raced north. He was too late to join forces with the brother earls, Edwin and Morcar, whose fyrd was defeated at Fulford on 20 September, but he arrived sooner than the Norwegians expected and surprised them on 25 September at Stamford Bridge. If there were ever any doubts about Harold's military skills, those doubts were dispelled by the Battle of Stamford Bridge. The mightiest warrior in the northern hemisphere and the most dangerous threat to England's independence were defeated and destroyed in the greatest victory ever won by an English army over the Scandinavians. Harald Hardrada, Tostig and ninety per cent of their soldiers were slaughtered. After the truce, the Norwegian survivors could man only twenty-four of their longships. Yet there was irony in Harold's triumph: the portent of Halley's comet was not to be denied by the prowess of a king. The Norwegian survivors sailed home as easily as they had come, before a fresh breeze from the south. The wind had changed.

On 28 September the Norman army landed unopposed at Pevensey in Sussex. When the news reached York, Harold rode south with his housecarls and those of his thegns who were mounted, leaving Edwin and Morcar to follow as soon as they could with a newly-levied northern fyrd. After pausing in London to assemble more soldiers from south-eastern England, he set out for Duke William's headquarters at Hastings on 11 October. Some of his commanders advised him to wait until the arrival of the northern and western fyrds gave him numerical superiority, but Harold was determined to protect the people of Sussex from the ravages of invaders. On the evening of 13 October he advanced to establish a position on the hill at Senlac.

PREVIOUS PAGES King Harold (left) is struck down and killed by a Norman knight at the battle of Hastings; a scene from the Bayeux Tapestry. The tapestry, which depicts the conquest, was used to decorate the nave of Bayeux cathedral. It was probably made in England and may have been commissioned by King William I's half-brother, Odo, bishop of Bayeux.

The coast of Sussex has silted since 1066. Hastings was then on the southern tip of a peninsula, with bays on either side, into which streams ran through thick marshes from the base of Senlac Hill. The only way out of the peninsula by land lay over that hill, and below its brow, where the marshes protected his flanks, Harold drew up his army in a single line from stream to stream, nine or ten ranks deep, with housecarls forming the front rank and surrounding the king in the centre. If William did not want to withdraw to the sea and attempt a landing elsewhere, he had no alternative but to attack this formidable position.

On the morning of 14 October William chose to give battle. As they advanced into the valley in front of Harold, the Norman soldiers were inevitably disorganized, and consequently vulnerable. But Harold did not exploit their disadvantage: he remained in his position and allowed them to form their line of battle about 200 yards ahead of him. The armies were roughly equal in numbers, each being about 7,000

The death of King Harald Hardrada at the battle of Stamford Bridge on 25 September, 1066, from *La Estoire de Seint Aedward.* The thirteenth-century artist has depicted the armour and methods of his own time; in fact both armies fought on foot.

43

strong, and their armour was almost identical. But their weapons and methods were different: all the long-haired Saxons fought on foot with axes and javelins, while among the Normans, whose short, round, Latin hair-cuts had led the people of Sussex to believe that William had landed with an army of monks, there were cavalry, infantry and archers, some of whom were armed with the new European crossbows, which the popes were later to ban as barbarous.

In the centre of his army William commanded the Normans, with the French and Flemish on his right and the Bretons on his left. At about nine in the morning he ordered his archers forward and, when they failed to have any impact on the housecarls' shields, he ordered a general advance of his infantry. On his left the Bretons hesitated under a barrage of javelins, then broke and fled down the hill, colliding with their archers and cavalry, who became bogged down in the marsh. Before the Bretons could check their confusion, some of the ranks on the English right set out after them, and seeing their flank threatened, the rest of William's infantry fell back. With his half-brother Odo and Count Eustace, William rode out to rally the centre and right. As a bishop, Odo was forbidden to shed blood, but he overcame the restriction by carrying a mace, with which he battered his enemies senseless. When the centre and right had regrouped, William detached some of his Norman knights, who charged across to the left and almost annihilated the English who had been slaughtering the Bretons. Then, with his flank regained, William advanced his cavalry. His knights reached the English line and remained ineffectively engaged with the wall of shields for some time, but eventually the Normans in the centre began to fall back slowly. Again some of the English ranks gave chase, and again they were cut to pieces by a cavalry charge in their flank, this time led by William himself.

After the battle, the Normans claimed that their withdrawals had been intentional. Some modern historians have discounted the claim as the idle boast of men who were ashamed of their retreat, and argue that soldiers who have been committed to the attack can not easily change their direction. But this depends on the extent of their commitment, which, in the earlier case of the Bretons, was slight. It would not have been so difficult for the

OPPOSITE Three Norman knights; a twelfth-century bronze fragment, probably part of a casket, known as the Temple Pyx.

45

Normans to withdraw if they had practised it and knew in advance that they were going to do it. The fact which this argument ignores is that the feigned retreat was a regular Breton and Norman tactic. Originating among the ancient nomad horsemen of the steppes, the tactic had been introduced into Brittany by the Alans who fled from the Huns to settle there in the fifth century. The Bretons had used it many times during the 200 years before the Battle of Hastings, and the Normans had been so impressed by it that they had adopted it, practised it in their peacetime manoeuvres and used it effectively themselves on several occasions – most recently at the Battle of Arques in 1053.

However, whether the retreats were intentional or not, their consequence was the same. The casualties suffered in the defeat of their counter-attacks so reduced the English numbers that they were forced to shorten their line. At either end there was now a gap of solid ground between the flank and the marsh. In a last bid for victory before nightfall, William ordered his entire army to advance. While the front of the English line held, William's cavalry charged through the gaps and bore down on

Duke William, Bishop Odo and Count Eustace rallying the Normans at Hastings. On the left, Odo brandishes his mace; while on the right, Eustace points to William, who has raised his helmet, to reassure the knights that he has not been killed.

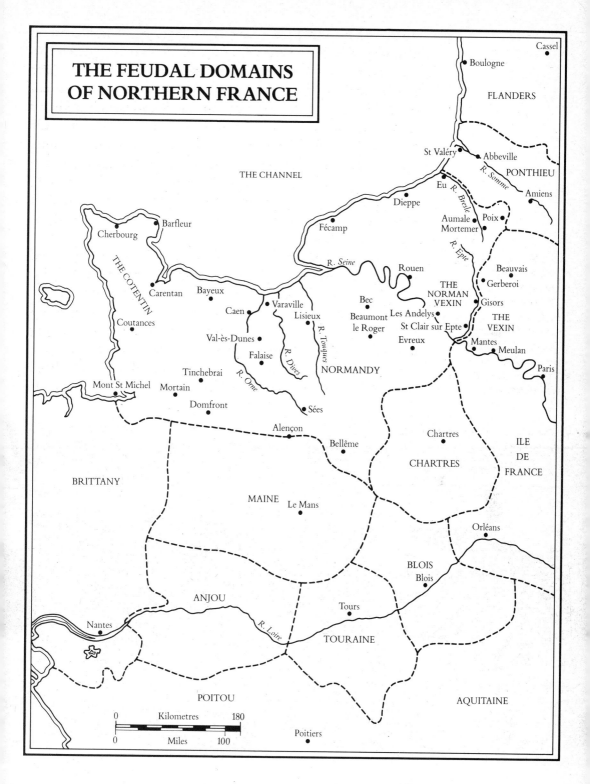

THE FEUDAL DOMAINS
OF NORTHERN FRANCE

Cassel

Boulogne

FLANDERS

THE CHANNEL

St Valéry
Abbeville
R. Somme
PONTHIEU

Eu
R. Bresle
Dieppe
Amiens

Barfleur
Cherbourg

Fécamp
Aumale
Poix
Mortemer

R. Epte

THE COTENTIN

R. Seine
Rouen
Beauvais
Gerberoi

Carentan
Bayeux
THE NORMAN VEXIN
Gisors

Caen
Varaville
Bec
Les Andelys
THE VEXIN

Coutances
Lisieux
Beaumont le Roger
St Clair sur Epte
Mantes

Val-ès-Dunes
R. Touques
Evreux
Meulan

Falaise
R. Dives
Paris

Mont St Michel
Tinchebrai
R. Orne
NORMANDY

Mortain
Domfront
Sées

Alençon
Chartres
ILE DE FRANCE

Bellême
CHARTRES

BRITTANY

MAINE
Le Mans

Orléans

BLOIS
Blois

ANJOU
Tours

Nantes
R. Loire
TOURAINE

POITOU

AQUITAINE

| 0 | Kilometres | 180 |
| 0 | Miles | 100 |

Poitiers

Warfare in the Eleventh Century

In spite of their common Scandinavian origins, the Saxon and Norman armies were entirely different in their methods. The Saxons fought on foot, they made little effective use of their archers, and their principal formation was a thick phalanx, known as the shield-wall. The Normans, on the other hand, were all cavalry – Duke William's archers and infantry were mercenaries or allies. Although the Saxons could withstand a head-on charge, the Normans could out-manoeuvre them. After the conquest, when knights fought on foot beside fyrdsmen and archers were used to better effect, the Anglo-Norman army became as versatile as it was formidable.

LEFT A Saxon soldier wielding his battle axe, from a twelfth-century manuscript.

RIGHT A Norman knight in his hauberk, from the church of Saint Martial in Limoges.

BELOW Norman knights charging at Hastings and raising their light lances to throw them like javelins – a technique they acquired from their Breton neighbours. A section of the Bayeux Tapestry.

Apres seynt Edward reg
na Harald le fiz Gode
wyn count de kent. a for
ea tort. ix. moys. dunk ve
en wilk bastard. e ly tol
yst la vye e le regne e cquist
la tere. harald gist a walthm

Post regna will vai
mid xxi. an. puis mo
rust e gist a kame en
smundpe.

its flanks. From each end Harold's army crumbled towards the centre until Norman knights broke through the housecarls, and the king, who may already have been wounded in the eye, was cut down beneath his standard. The remnants of the routed fyrd fled, and the survivors of the housecarls fell back to the ditch where they made their final, futile stand.

Before the last attack William had never been near to victory, but Harold had made the mistakes: he had engaged unnecessarily before his overwhelming strength was assembled; he had failed to attack when his enemy was exposed and disorganized; he had allowed some of his soldiers to counter-attack too soon; and by staying to the end with his housecarls he had left his kingdom leaderless. His tragic flaw was his audacity; at Stamford Bridge it had brought him triumph, but at Hastings it cost him an army and his life – and it cost England its freedom.

After waiting for five days for submissions that never came, William marched north-east along the coast, garrisoning the ports to secure his communications across the Channel. From Dover, where he was joined by Norman reinforcements, he marched inland to Canterbury. Sickness among his soldiers, to which he succumbed himself, delayed William in Canterbury for four weeks, but during that time forlorn representatives from the south-eastern towns, including the ancient capital of Wessex at Winchester, came at last with their eager submissions, in the words of the Norman poet Guy of Amiens, 'like flies to a running sore'. From London, however, there was no sign of submission. The city was divided: some loyal Saxons had persuaded a section of the Witan to elect Edgar the Atheling as Harold's successor, but Edwin and Morcar, who had arrived with their fyrd, had not sworn allegiance to him, although they had agreed to support him against the Normans; and Archbishop Stigand and Esegar, the Sheriff of Middlesex, who had been carried wounded from the field at Hastings, were corresponding secretly with the Norman Duke in the hope that they might be allowed to retain their offices.

At the beginning of November, William marched west as far as Winchester, turned north to cross the Thames at Wallingford into Oxfordshire, where Stigand offered his submission, and then turned east round the north of London, separating the city

OPPOSITE A fourteenth-century representation of the battle of Hastings, suggesting that King Harold was killed by Duke William.

51

from Edwin and Morcar, who had apparently withdrawn their fyrd northwards on his approach. Isolated, defenceless and threatened with famine by the systematic devastation that had accompanied William's circular march, London surrendered. When William reached Little Berkhampstead, bishops, leading citizens and Edgar the Atheling came out to offer him the crown.

On Christmas Day 1066 the coronation took place in Westminster Abbey. It was a dramatic ceremony. When the traditional shout of acclamation rang from the Abbey, the Norman guards thought that their duke was in danger, and being trained soldiers they created a diversion by setting fire to the neighbouring buildings. While the final rituals were hurriedly concluded, the startled congregation fled into the chaos of the streets.

Once he had been crowned, William began to restore order to as much of the kingdom as he had conquered. Further pillage was forbidden; the citizens of London were given a charter confirming their privileges; and, content for the time being to exact only tolerable ransoms, William offered a pardon to all Saxons who had not fought beside Harold. In response to this offer, thegns from central and northern England came to make their submission at William's headquarters in Barking, and among them, according to the Norman chronicler William of Poitiers, were Edwin and Morcar. The *Anglo-Saxon Chronicle* records that the brother earls had already submitted at the same time as Edgar the Atheling, but William of Malmesbury wrote that they had by then withdrawn, and it seems most likely that he and William of Poitiers are right. If the earls had been in London when William reached Little Berkhampstead, the city would not have been defenceless, and they would hardly have made their hollow submission until their vital fyrd had been dispersed to safety. King William received Edwin and Morcar cordially and even suggested that Edwin should marry one of his daughters, but the earls were confined to his court as captive guests, and when he returned to Normandy soon afterwards they, Edgar, Stigand and several other earls were among the hostages that accompanied him.

Before leaving to attend to the affairs of his duchy, William delegated the government of southern England to his half-

E dimence viii.
sour du mois
Octobre ensieu
uant lan de gra
ce m.iiii.lxxi. Le
ducs guillaume
fut a tresgrant solempnite par
les prelatz z hault barons dangle
terre couronne oinct et sacre a wy
a westmonstier emprez londres.
Apree son couronnement
il demoura sur le paie enquerat

de lestre des gens qui parauant
auoient fait serment de le tenir
a wy apree le trespas du bon roy
edouard et senestoient pariurez
mais par sa misericorde le pardo
na atous. Apree ceulx qui encel
le sa conqueste lauoient serui
auv aucune donna deniers.
Auv autree il fist auoir en ma
riauge aucunes nobles dames
du puis heritiere de thane ter
res a cause de leure marie qui

Chepstow castle, one of
the earliest stone castles in
Britain. The keep was
built by William Fitz
Osbern between
1067–1072 and heightened
between 1220–1245.

The head of William I on a silver penny, minted at Dover.

brother Odo, whom he created Earl of Kent, and gave control over all the country north of the Thames to the new Earl of Hereford, William Fitz Osbern. But during his absence the oppression of these governors soon roused the English to their first resistance. The men of Hereford raided round the new castle, while the Norman garrison watched helplessly from the wooden walls, and the men of Kent – having found themselves an unlikely ally in Count Eustace of Boulogne, who was indignant because he had not been better rewarded for his services at Hastings – besieged Dover Castle until Eustace abandoned them after the garrison's first sally. Nevertheless, by the time William returned at the beginning of December 1067, Archbishop Aldred of York had formed a substantial English party which was prepared to support William as the only ruler capable of maintaining order. Early in the following year William was able to leave the peaceful south-east and march into the farthest reaches of Wessex, where Harold's mother and

The reverse side of a penny was always stamped with a cross, so that the coin could be clipped into halves and quarters.

bastard sons had found refuge among the loyal thegns who had only been excluded from the Hastings campaign by Harold's speed. With an army in which for the first time Saxon soldiers served beside his French mercenaries, William laid siege to Exeter. The city fell at the end of eighteen days, but by then Harold's family had escaped, and during the next two years, a nuisance rather than a threat, his sons raided the west coast with a fleet that they had raised in Dublin.

After the fall of Exeter, Devon and Cornwall submitted, then Gloucester and Bristol followed their example, and by Whitsun William had returned to London with the south-west subdued, only to discover that the north had risen in its place. Three of his hostages had absconded: Edwin and Morcar were levying the fyrd in Mercia, and in Northumbria a Saxon called Gospatric, to whom William had sold the earldom of Bernicia, was attempting to raise a rebellion in favour of Edgar the Atheling. The risings were premature and half-hearted. On William's

57

approach the Mercian thegns returned to their homes, and by the time he reached York, Gospatric and Edgar had fled to charitable refuge at the court of the King of Scots, Malcolm Canmore, the conqueror of Macbeth, who was in love with Edgar's saintly sister Margaret.

Since he was wary of the devotion that their names seemed to inspire among Saxon thegns, William pardoned Edwin and Morcar, but their power was curtailed by the many castles which were hurriedly built throughout the north with forced labour, and by the French commanders who were granted estates in the once autonomous earldoms. After quartering a garrison and building the foundations of a castle at York, William marched south, initiating the construction of further castles as he went. The suppression of the west and north had been easier than he could have hoped. On his return from the west he felt secure enough to bring Matilda over from Normandy and have her crowned as his Queen. But the risings of 1068 had been as ineffective as they were ill-prepared; a dangerous year was to follow.

The first revolts of 1069 were limited. Outraged by the indiscriminate slaughter that had been perpetrated by the northern commander, Robert de Commines, and his soldiers, Northumbrians broke into their quarters at Durham by night, murdered the soldiers in their beds and set fire to the bishop's house, burning Robert to death in the flames. Then the men of York rallied around a small army that had come south with Edgar the Atheling and laid siege to the castle. Again William marched north, surprising the besiegers. Again Edgar fled to Scotland and again, after ordering a second castle to be built outside York's walls, William returned to the south.

But for some time the predominantly Scandinavian people of north-eastern England had been negotiating secretly with King Swein of Denmark, and, at the end of August, Swein made his bid for the throne of England. In a fleet of 240 longships commanded by Swein's brother and sons, a Danish army sailed up the east coast and landed in the Humber, where it was joined by Edgar, Gospatric, Earl Waltheof of Huntingdon and many other formerly pro-Norman thegns. At last the men of north-eastern England rose in formidable numbers to support them. By the end of September York had been burned to the ground,

NORMAN ENGLAND

the castles had been rased, the survivors of the Norman garrison were prisoners in Danish ships and Archbishop Aldred had died of a broken heart.

The news inspired new risings in the south-west, but William left these to his subordinate commanders and for the third time marched north. From York the Danes and their allies had withdrawn to a defensive position on the Humber, and as William was advancing to attack them he learned that the Mercians had risen on his south-western flank. Leaving his half-brother Robert with a small corps to watch the enemy on the Humber, William marched into Mercia and routed the rebels at Stafford. On his way back to the Humber, however, he received news from Robert warning him that the Anglo-Danish army was returning to York. His attempt to reach the city before them was thwarted by another group of English rebels, who destroyed the only bridge over the River Aire and delayed him for three weeks until he found an undefended ford. As he had done against London, William marched round York, devastating the farms as he went; and, as it had been before, the tactic was successful. Around the isolated and unfortified ruins the farms were empty, and within them the contents of the once-rich granaries were ashes. Knowing that they could not hope to withstand a siege, the Danish commanders withdrew the bulk of their army before it was too late and sent messengers to sue for peace.

Once the remains of York had been recaptured, William was generous to the rebel leaders and the invaders: as they made their submission one by one he pardoned the English commanders; he did not pursue the hapless Edgar, who once again fled to Scotland; and he allowed the Danes to shelter their fleet on the Humber for the winter, and apparently bribed them to remain inactive. But he was determined that the common people of the north would never dare to defy him again. During most of November and December, William's soldiers destroyed every town, village and house between York and Durham, slaughtering every human being they could find. After spending Christmas at York they administered the same punishment so effectively to Stafford, Derby and Chester that Gerbod, the new Earl of Chester, soon tired of his desolate, indigent earldom and went home disappointed to Flanders.

The south-western risings were suppressed by the subordinate commanders and the 'Harrying of the North' achieved
its cruel purpose. On his return to Winchester at Easter William
paid off most of his mercenaries. But there was still one pocket
of resistance, which was to be remembered more for the legends
that it sired than its success. At the end of 1069, when the abbacy
of Peterborough on the edge of the rebellious Fen country fell
vacant, William appointed the Abbot of Malmesbury, Turold
of Fécamp, who, apart from his clerical qualifications, had

The Norman *motte*
(mound) and bailey (outer
wall) of Skipsea castle,
near Bridlington in
Yorkshire.

61

demonstrated a certain prowess as a soldier. At the news of the appointment, a group of local inhabitants naively invited some of the Danes to help them resist the warrior abbot. When the Danes agreed, a stocky, agile, golden-haired thegn called Hereward the Wake guided them back through the fens. But the Danes did not defend Peterborough: they stripped the abbey of all its splendid treasures and, when Turold arrived with too few knights to challenge them, they persuaded him to let them leave peacefully with their plunder.

Abandoned by their worthless allies but certain that they would never be pardoned for their part in the pillage of an abbey, Hereward and his supporters took refuge in a fortified camp on the Isle of Ely and held out until, in 1071, Edwin and Morcar left William's court to join them. While recruiting an army, Edwin was murdered by his own supporters, but Morcar reached Ely with a small force. The threat was enough to bring William himself to suppress it. After several bloody assaults, the stronghold was taken. Morcar was captured and remained a closely-guarded prisoner for the rest of his life, but Hereward escaped and, although he seems to have remained at large, disappeared from the certain records of history. Like the stories of his early life, Hereward's subsequent adventures were recounted only in ballads.

Against what seemed to be impossible odds, William had conquered England through his own determination, consistent and extraordinary good luck, and the division and incompetence of his enemies. By 1072 the only threat to his sovereignty lay beyond the northern border, where King Malcolm had at last persuaded Margaret to marry him and might therefore be expected to take a greater interest in the pretensions of his brother-in-law Edgar. After a pre-emptive show of strength, in which William led his army to the Firth of Forth, the two kings concluded a treaty at Abernethy. Malcolm received estates in northern England – for which he paid homage – gave William his eldest son, Duncan, as a hostage and agreed to expel Edgar the Atheling from his kingdom.

When Edgar eventually made his peace with William, William pardoned him and gave him a pension. He could afford to be generous: the charming but simple-minded young Saxon pretender had never been more than a puppet in the northern

Malcolm Canmore, King of Scots, and his queen, Saint Margaret, from a sixteenth-century manuscript. (Ms. Wood C. 9.)

risings, and he was too little-known to be well supported. The only man with the authority and influence to rally the English people in a united defence had fallen at Hastings. In most of England they had fought for Harold because he and the brothers who were captured or killed beside him were their earls, and in Mercia and Northumbria they had fought for him because their earls were his allies. Once he was gone there was no focus for their resistance. They might fight for the freedom of their shire out of parochial self-interest, or for a surviving thegn out of duty, but, in a kingdom that the rivalry of the earls had long divided, they had not yet learned to fight for England.

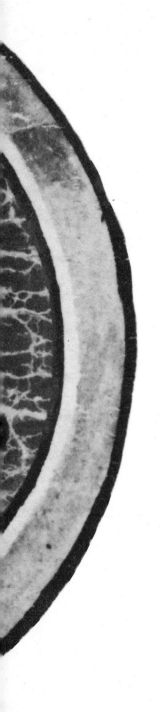

3 A Feudal Kingdom

AFTER 1072 THE ENGLISH were comparatively passive. During the last fifteen years of his reign, King William spent much of his time in his duchy, leaving the administration of his kingdom to regents and in particular to his one trusted friend, Lanfranc. The exiled Archbishop Robert of Jumièges was dead, and in 1070 Lanfranc had inevitably replaced his usurper Stigand as Archbishop of Canterbury. Under the rule of a king who was also Duke of Normandy, England was drawn into the tide of feudal rivalries that made up the world of European politics, and the wealth of the conquered land became the resource with which William defended his continental domains.

William maintained that he was the rightful heir to Edward, but he treated his kingdom more like a prize than an inheritance; and, unlike Cnut, he did not intend to leave it as he had found it. If the English thought that he might, they were to learn all too soon that they were wrong. To William, the English had forfeited everything in defeat: their land and their property were his to distribute as he wished. As his suppression of resistance progressed, the estates of dispossessed English landlords were divided among his followers. Since the suppression was piecemeal, the distribution of land was also piecemeal; although great barons were rewarded with many manors, those manors were scattered throughout the kingdom, and the only unified estates were the palatinates, which were created on the borders and threatened coast so that the few barons who had been entrusted with their defence might have the authority and manpower to fulfil their duty.

The old order was swept away, the old earldoms were eroded or broken up, and in their place William imposed a new landed hierarchy that was modelled on the rigid feudal society of France. In principle all the land belonged to the king; the great barons were only tenants-in-chief, holding their estates in the fee of 'knights' service', by which they were required to provide the king with varying quotas of knights for up to forty days in each year. With this contract William retained the rights of a universal landlord and supplemented the fyrd with a reliable and experienced corps of cavalry. But to the tenants-in-chief, most of whom could command more men than their quotas required, the obligation was hardly onerous. Their

PREVIOUS PAGES William the Conqueror, from a genealogical tree made at the end of the thirteenth-century.

quotas were easily filled by the chain of lesser barons and knights to whom they sub-let manors in return for the same military service; in addition they dominated the indigenous inhabitants of their new estates with permanent retinues of professional landless knights, who manned the menacing wooden castles that they were soon to replace with more enduring stone memorials to the Norman occupation.

Some thegns and freemen became the humblest tenants, paying a proportion of their produce to the Norman knight of the manor in return for a part of their former freehold, while others were reduced to the level of serfs, working beside them in the fields and owing their master as much of their labour and possessions as he cared to demand. They were so much his property in the eyes of the law that they could even be sold to pay his debts. On the royal manors which William retained in every shire, the humblest English subjects were less exploited than on many baronial estates, and their limited legal rights were more often respected. But this was merely a matter of judicious policy – the king was as capable of indifference as any rapacious baron. His extension of royal forests and his introduction of forest laws, by which men could be mutilated for taking his game, led to more widespread and lasting resentment than suffering. Nevertheless, the wretched families who were evicted from the sixty Hampshire villages that were rased in order to extend the New Forest can hardly have managed to smile at the irony of the Peterborough chronicler, who wrote of William: 'He loved the tall deer as if he were their father.'

In the border palatinates the new earls were allowed to exercise many of the royal prerogatives, but throughout the rest of the kingdom William's power became even more pervasive than it was in Normandy. Since the estates of his magnates were scattered, he was the largest landlord within each shire, and the government of the shires, which began to be known also as counties, was delegated to newly appointed sheriffs, who lived on the royal estates during their tenure of office and ruled with all the authority of the viscounts in Normandy. Control over the administration of temporal justice was restored to the Crown: in the shire courts, from which the earls were excluded, the sheriffs usually sat alone without the bishops; and even the

The Feudal Economy

The economy of Norman England was predominantly agricultural. Grain was grown on almost every acre that could be ploughed, and cattle were grazed in fens and woodlands. At first, the former freeholders of the Danelaw paid their rents with crippling proportions of their produce, and elsewhere tenants devoted so much time to cultivating their lords' estates that they had little left to provide for their families. But, with the growth in population and the increasing use of money, the burden of feudal dues diminished. Barons began to collect the rents of richer tenants in cash and pay casual labourers with loaves and herrings. By the middle of the twelfth century, most villeins had enough sons to till their own land as well as their masters, and a man might hold nine acres for as little as 'is. 6d. and two hens at Christmas'.

RIGHT An early eleventh-century drawing of a Saxon farmer with a plough and an axe. (Ms. Junius 11, f. 54.)

BELOW Norman farmers ploughing, sowing and harvesting, from the Bayeux Tapestry.

TOP Saxon farmers chopping wood, from an eleventh-century calendar.

ABOVE Farmers reaping, from an eleventh-century calendar.

Dux Romanorum Wills et validorum
Rex est Anglorum bello conquestor eorum

Willo Conquestor Anglie genuit de Alienora regina

Robtin
Curte
hose

Willm
Rufu

henric
regem

Adam
Comitissa
blesenc

Thebald
Comitiss
blesenc

Consta
na Comi
tissa bri
tannie

Stepha
ni
regis

Conquestor regnauit xxi annis xi mensib3 Cadamo iacet

William the Conqueror
and his barons, from a
fourteenth-century
manuscript.

LEFT A fourteenth-century
genealogical tree of
William the Conqueror
and his Norman
successors.

71

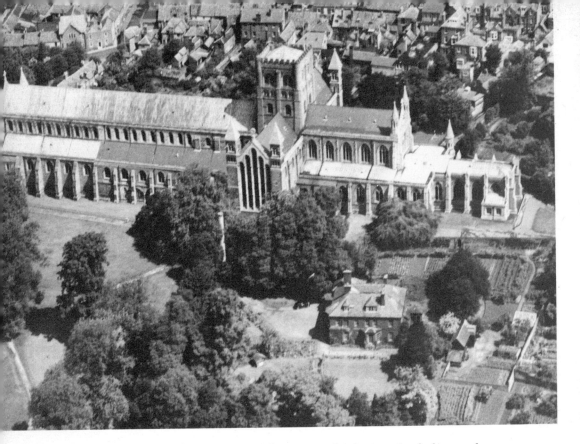

The Benedictine abbey at Saint Albans, which was begun in 1077 and became a cathedral in 1877. The square tower was built with bricks from the Roman ruin at Verulamium.

OPPOSITE The interior of Saint Albans cathedral.

private manorial courts, which exercised almost the same petty jurisdiction as the courts of the hundreds, were supervised by the newly-instituted special commissioners, who investigated the conduct of all temporal courts and assessed the royal revenues in each shire. William was practical, he adopted everything English that was useful and introduced only those measures which he thought necessary to contain his new subjects or control his barons. Yet the result of his diligence was a transformation: ruling directly through the sheriffs and special commissioners and indirectly through the feudal contract with his barons, he turned England into a single administrative unit, established the foundations of an efficient royal bureaucracy and made himself master of an advanced feudal society which lacked all the anarchic flaws that were crippling its continental counterparts.

In accordance with the expectations of Pope Alexander II, and in keeping with their own convictions, William and Lanfranc reformed and reorganized the English Church. Monasteries were founded, some bishops' sees were transferred to larger towns, and as on the land, so in the church French

replaced English until, by the end of William's reign, there were only two English bishops in the kingdom. The spiritual jurisdiction which bishops and archdeacons had only been able to exercise through the temporal courts was withdrawn to new ecclesiastical courts, which were answerable to the synod that sat regularly under Lanfranc, and the Church in England received the same legislative and judicial independence that it enjoyed in Latin Europe.

During his tenure of the see of Canterbury, Lanfranc revealed talents for diplomacy, administration and politics which were at least equal to his talent for teaching. For all his piety, enthusiasm for monasticism and instinctive obedience to Rome, his loyalty to William in the last resort was stronger than his commitment to the Hildebrandine reforms. When Hildebrand succeeded Alexander II as Pope Gregory VII in 1073, he issued a decree forbidding clerical marriages and declaring those that existed null and void. Then he recklessly issued two more decrees claiming feudal suzerainty over nearly every crown in Europe and passing a sentence of excommunication upon anyone who conferred or received an ecclesiastical benefice by lay investiture. The first decree was adopted by Lanfranc, although with the enlightened reservation that the existing marriages of English parish priests should remain valid. But to the second, William answered respectfully that he would pay no homage that had not been paid by his predecessors. In answer to the third decree Lanfranc went to Rome in person and, arguing that the English kings had always had special privileges, persuaded the Pope to compromise by allowing William to invest his own bishops for the rest of his reign.

Although William and Lanfranc were successful in their defiance, and although they continued to recognize Gregory's spiritual suzerainty and even flattered him occasionally by consulting him on temporal matters, their once cordial relationship with the papacy was soured. When Gregory's presumptuous zeal brought him into armed conflict with the Holy Roman Emperor, England remained neutral; and, in a letter to a legate of the anti-Pope Clement, Lanfranc later remarked that the Emperor's capture of Rome might be seen as a sign that heaven was on his side.

Once he had conquered England, William did not continue

OPPOSITE Norman soldiers on board a ship, from a contemporary manuscript.

75

Ego Willimus cognoie Bastardus Rex Anglie
Do et concedo tibi nepoti meo Alano Bri
tannie Comiti et heredibus tuis impetui om
nes villas et tras que nup fuerunt Comitis
Edwyn in Eboraeshira cu feodis militu et
salijs et alijs libtate et consuetudinibus ita
libe et honorifice sicut idem Edwinus ea
tenuit. Dat in obsidione coram Ci
tate Eboraci.

his invasion into the rest of Britain. Although the Welsh, who had supported eastern rebels, the Irish, who had supported Harold's bastards, and the Scots, who continued to raid across the border, had all given him adequate justification for campaigns, William had no alternative but to consolidate his gains and remain predominantly on the defensive. The earls of Shropshire and Hereford advanced his borders into Wales on their own volition and, in answer to the Scots' raids, a counter-raid reached Falkirk. But for the rest of William's reign his French domains were disrupted by rebellions and his Norman borders were threatened by Flanders, Anjou and France. If he had divided his military resources between these enemies and a further British offensive, he would have risked losing everything.

The alliance with Flanders broke down in 1071. William's father-in-law had two sons, Baldwin and Robert, and, on his death in 1067, he was succeeded as Count of Flanders by the elder, Baldwin VI, who in turn was succeeded by his own elder son, Arnulf, in 1070. Since Arnulf was a child, William allowed his valued Norman viceroy, William Fitz Osbern, to quit his post and serve as the young count's guardian. But when Arnulf's uncle Robert raised an army and in the following year seized the county for himself, killing both guardian and ward at the Battle of Cassel, William justifiably refused to recognize him as the rightful count and rashly supported the regular but unsuccessful attacks of Arnulf's brother. Soon afterwards, there was a dangerous rebellion in Maine, which was supported by Count Fulk of Anjou, and in which the Norman garrison was expelled from Le Mans. Although Le Mans surrendered to William's Anglo-Norman army in 1073, the county was never entirely pacified and, to keep Fulk from interfering, William was forced to agree that his eldest son, Robert, whom he appointed Count of Maine, should recognize Fulk as his overlord. In the west, relations with Brittany alternated between inconclusive war and faithless peace until 1086, when Count Alan of Brittany married William's daughter Constance.

There was even a Norman rebellion in England. To William's barons the new feudal kingdom was a bitter disappointment. They had hoped to enjoy the same freedom

OPPOSITE King William investing his son-in-law, Count Alan of Brittany, with lands that had been appropriated from the Saxon Earl Edwin of Mercia, from a fifteenth-century manuscript. (Ms. Lyell 22, f. 6v.)

King Philip I of France,
from a fourteenth-century
manuscript.

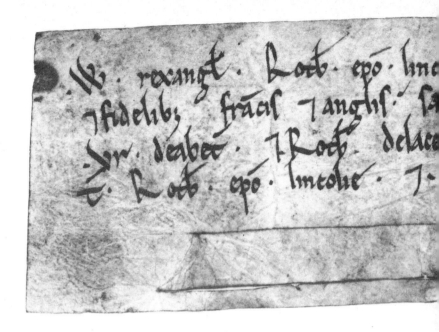

and privileges as their peers in France and instead they had found themselves weakened by their widespread estates, restrained by the authority of the sheriffs and inhibited by the curiosity of the special commissioners. At first their survival in a conquered land depended on unity and loyalty to their commander, but so successful were William's suppression and reorganization that, as early as 1075, two of the younger generation felt secure enough to quarrel over the spoils. While William was in Normandy, Earl Roger of Hereford and Earl Ralph of Norfolk planned a *coup*. They obtained a promise of support from Denmark and, with the enticement of the English throne, they persuaded the last powerful Englishman, Earl Waltheof of Huntingdon, to join them. Waltheof soon changed his mind, however, and reported the plot to Lanfranc. By the time the Danes arrived, the rebels' French mercenaries had been defeated by English fyrds, and contenting themselves with a brief raid, the Danes left England for the last time. Ralph escaped to join other malcontents in Brittany, but Roger was captured and stood trial for treason with the protesting Waltheof, whose brief but repented lapse of loyalty had given William a chance to get rid of him. On their conviction they were sentenced to the separate penalties prescribed by the laws

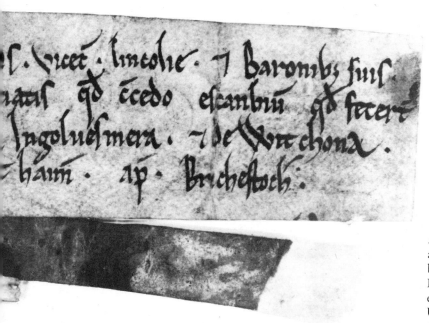

A writ of King William I, addressed to 'his faithful barons French and English', authorizing the exchange of land between Urse d'Abetot and Robert de Lacy.

of Normandy and of England: Roger spent the rest of his life in prison, and Waltheof was executed.

The fate of the rebels in England served as a salutary warning, and thereafter the only leading barons who dared to defy William were members of his own family. Before leaving for England in 1066, William had nominally invested his eldest son, Robert, with the duchy of Normandy, but even after Robert had been invested with the county of Maine in 1073, when he was nineteen years old, William had refused to allow him any part in the government of either province. Resentful and openly defiant, Robert was eventually expelled from the duchy and, joining forces with some of the discontented subjects of Maine and Brittany, he sought assistance from King Philip of France.

The envious and ineffectual French king had been a child while William was invading England and his guardian had been William's father-in-law, but as soon as he had become free to do so he had provided men and money for William's enemies. Delighted by the opportunity to divide the ducal house in civil war, Philip allowed Robert to garrison his rebels in the border castle of Gerberoi, from which they could make raids into Normandy. But his fear of William got the better of him when William came in person to lay siege to the castle. He changed

sides and sent soldiers to support William, although the support was intentionally too small to ensure William's victory. Gerberoi withstood the siege. In a skirmish outside the walls, father and son actually met in single combat: William was wounded in the hand, his horse was killed beneath him, and the anxious Norman barons were only saved from the embarrassment of patricide by an English thegn called Tokig of Wallingford, who leapt from his saddle and gave his mount to his king. Humiliated, William withdrew from Gerberoi, leaving his barons to negotiate a reconciliation, but he made no compromise, and soon afterwards Robert was again a belligerent exile.

The other rebellious kinsman was William's ambitious and ostentatious half-brother Odo, Bishop of Bayeux and Earl of Kent. In 1082, in defiance of the law against levying troops within the realm, Odo raised an army, ostensibly to support the Pope in his war with the Holy Roman Emperor, although some said that his real purpose was to seize the papacy for himself. William ordered his immediate arrest and imprisonment, and when Odo protested that as a bishop he could not be arrested, William, prompted by Lanfranc, answered dialectically that he was arresting him not as Bishop of Bayeux, but as Earl of Kent.

Towards the end of William's reign, in 1085, a threat arose which was expected to be even more dangerous than the combined rebellions and invasion of 1069. Reports reached England that Swein's son, King Cnut IV of Denmark, who had already made one attempted invasion of England in support of the Norman rebels, was preparing another with the help of Count Robert of Flanders, and that their fleet was larger than any that had yet sailed against the shores of England. The invasion never materialized – Cnut was assassinated and the plan was abandoned. But by this time William had decided to raise the Danegeld to pay for the mercenaries whom he had imported to reinforce his fyrd and feudal cavalry; and he had approached the task with the same efficiency that had already revitalized other English institutions. To discover exactly how much each man could afford to pay, William empowered the special commissioners to question landlords and tenants under oath and ordered their findings to be recorded in a book that was later to be known as the Domesday Book.

OPPOSITE King Philip I of France with his court, from an eleventh-century manuscript. 'Fond of nothing but good cheer and sleep', Philip ruled for forty-eight years and, although he took advantage of every quarrel, did little more than hold his own against the expanding power of Normandy.

83

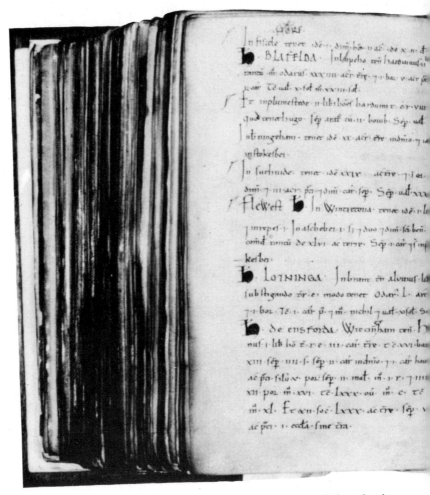

Throughout 1086 the commissioners collected details about each manor, ranging from its size and value through the numbers of tenants, serfs and livestock to the number of fishponds and even the number of ploughs. 'So narrowly did he cause the survey to be made', wrote the Anglo-Saxon chronicler, 'that there was not one single hide nor rood of land, nor – it is shameful to tell but he thought it no shame to do – was there an ox, cow or swine that was not set down in the writ.' The surviving Domesday Book is incomplete: the four most northern shires do not appear to have been covered, and some towns are missing, including London and Winchester, where the survey was collated and condensed. Nevertheless, it was the most comprehensive survey of its kind and it must have been compiled for many reasons other than the immediate need for

The Domesday Book.

Danegeld which prompted it. The value and extent of the king's estates were recorded in as much detail as others, and for the barons — most of whom had been granted their estates by word of mouth — copies of the relevant pages served subsequently in place of title deeds. The Domesday survey was an outstanding example of the Normans' thoroughness, and the book is still sombre evidence of the thoroughness of their expropriation of the English aristocracy and their retribution against English rebels: among the names of the tenants-in-chief there are very few that are English, and seventeen years after the 'Harrying of the North' many once-populous manors of northern Yorkshire were still so wasted and empty that the detailed Domesday Book could record them with three Latin words – *hoc est wasta*.

85

It is probable that William never saw the finished Domesday Book. While the survey was in progress he was still preparing for the expected invasion. On the first of August 1086, he held an enormous council in Salisbury, at which all the lesser barons, who were bound by feudal obligation only to the tenants-in-chief, were required to swear an overriding oath of allegiance directly to the king. But soon afterwards William learned that Cnut was dead, and by the end of the summer he had sailed for the last time from England.

Encouraged by King Philip, the citizens of Mantes in the French Vexin were making raids into Normandy. William retaliated by invading the French Vexin, claiming with some justification that it was his anyway, since it had been ceded to his father by Philip's father and then taken back while William was a child. In July 1087, the garrison of Mantes abandoned the town, setting fire to it as they left, and as William rode through the smouldering ruins, he fell. Some chroniclers say that he was overcome by exhaustion, others that his horse threw him against the pommel of his saddle, causing a haemorrhage in his massive stomach. So dire were the consequences that it seems more likely that he was injured. In agony and obviously dying, William was carried to his Norman capital at Rouen.

William's wife Matilda had died in 1083, his eldest son Robert was in exile, his second son Richard had been killed hunting and, of his five daughters, one was dead, two were in convents and two were married. But his third and favourite son, the pretentious, dissolute William Rufus, and his youngest son Henry were with the bishops and abbots that surrounded his deathbed.

Knowing that death was near, William bequeathed treasures to the poor and the Church and, at the instigation of his bishops, ordered the release of his eminent prisoners, including the earls Morcar of Northumbria, Roger of Hereford and Odo of Kent, although after his death all save Odo were returned to custody. Then, handing his crown and regalia to William Rufus, he ordered him to leave for England with the royal chaplain, to whom he entrusted a letter commending his chosen heir to Lanfranc. But there was no mention of Robert until the Archbishop of Rouen reminded the king that his eldest son had a right to the domains with which he had been endowed.

Eventually, after much recrimination, William grudgingly agreed that Robert should have Normandy and its dominions. 'I have forgiven him,' he said, 'let him not forgive himself so easily for bringing my old age with sorrow to the grave.' When there was no land left to bequeath, Henry approached his father's bed to receive no more than a promise of 5,000 pounds of silver. Bitterly disappointed, he left his father to spend his last hours with none but his clergy.

William died on 7 September 1087. He was buried in the abbey of Saint Stephen at Caen – which he had founded as a penance for his forbidden marriage – in a pitifully ill-attended ceremony that was as dramatic as his coronation had been. It was interrupted by a knight called Ascelin, who forbade the burial, claiming that the land on which the abbey had been built had belonged to his father and that he had received no payment for it. Once Ascelin had agreed to accept a compensation of sixty shillings, it was discovered that the stone sarcophagus was too small for the putrefying corpse. The body was broken and squeezed into it so tightly that the bowels burst. As the ceremony was hurriedly concluded, the attendants vainly piled incense into the burners, and the congregation choked in a disgusting stench.

Some Normans flattered William with fanciful eulogies, while the English chroniclers and even the half-Norman William of Malmesbury dwelt more on his ruthlessness and his greed. Although he was no more cruel than his contemporaries, he had ruled through fear; and although he was pious, he had been a hypocrite. If the Normans had honestly believed that he was the rightful heir to Edward, they might have thought twice about calling him 'the Conqueror'. Yet there must have been a side to William which the chroniclers did not see or did not choose to record – the side that in a profligate age was happily faithful to Matilda, and the side that was capable of lasting friendship with so admirable a man as Lanfranc. He had conquered England, reorganized its society and reformed its Church; the consequences of these achievements were to set him above other conquerors like Cnut in the subsequent pages of English history. But he was too short-sighted to foresee the consequences himself. Like his chosen heir's, his heart was in Normandy and his eyes were fixed no further than necessity or

87

The funeral of William I
and the coronation of his
son, William II, by
Archbishop Lanfranc,
from a fifteenth-century
manuscript.

the nearest and easiest gain. He had been very lucky to conquer England, he had reorganized it with little purpose other than to exploit it and, in his refusal to give his sons experience of government and in his division of his dominions, he had shown little care for the future. In a Europe that was weakened and divided by feudalism, feeble rulers and the war between the Papacy and the Holy Roman Empire, a united, rich and populous Anglo-Norman empire was the basis of a formidable power. But the only royal Norman to perceive its potential was Henry, the son to whom William had left none of it.

The stone slab marking the grave of William the Conqueror in the church of Saint Stephen at the Abbaye–aux–Hommes in Caen, which he founded as a penance for marrying Matilda of Flanders in defiance of the Pope.

4 'All That is Loathsome to God and Just Men'

On his deathbed William the Conqueror predicted that Normandy would be wretched under Robert. If he had not bequeathed it to him the outcome would almost certainly have been civil war, but the division of Normandy and England was every bit as dangerous. Nearly all the leading Norman families owned estates on both sides of the Channel, and their allegiance was therefore divided between their duke and their king. Their conduct, and in consequence the future of the two dominions, depended as much on their private interests as on the policies and personalities of their rulers.

Each of these rulers was to be remembered by a nickname. Robert was known as Curthose, perhaps because his legs were short, but more probably because he wore short breeches called *courte heuse*, which only reached below the knees, rather than the usual *heuse*, which stretched to the feet. William, whose face was flushed with dissipation, was known to the Normans as Le Roux and later to the English as Rufus. And 200 years after he died, Henry – who could read and write a bit better than his brothers, although not as well as a literate monk – was flatteringly christened Beauclerk.

They had inherited their father's love of hunting, his avarice and at least some of his skill in battle, but in other ways they were as different from him as they were from each other. Almost as soon as their father was dead, their separate characters became evident in the management of their inheritances. While England sensed the impending repression of William's impetuous despotism, Normandy under the gullible, irresolute Robert was reduced to anarchy, and, in the background, like a canny banker, the sly, calculating Henry made the best of his meagre legacy.

William II was about twenty-seven years old when he came to the throne of England. He was an unattractive man: he was of medium height, his body was heavy and ungainly, in his sneering face his wild grey and brown speckled eyes lay deep beneath a frowning forehead, he had a passionate temper and he stammered. In public, he affected the dignity and reserve that had been natural to his father, although his temper did not always allow him to maintain them. He was infatuated by all the brutal honour and formality of early chivalry, he admired great feats of arms, and his enthusiasm attracted military adventurers from all over Europe. But the knights in his retinue were so indulged that they could rape and plunder in their billets without fear of punishment. He surrounded himself with boisterous, debauched sycophants, and his private life was apparently disgraceful. Unfortunately the unanimous clerical chroniclers could not bring themselves to elaborate on the licentiousness that so outraged them, and it has to be admitted that they had many motives for wanting to blacken the king's name.

In his *Reign of William Rufus*, which was written during the

The Conqueror's eldest son, Robert Curthose, Duke of Normandy, from his tomb in Gloucester cathedral.

Hunting and Feasting

Hunting and feasting were the principal pastimes of the illiterate Saxon and Norman nobility. They were all devoted to their horses, hounds and hawks. But at table the Normans were more formal and reserved in their manners, and their ruthless extension of the royal game reserves caused widespread resentment.

LEFT An archer hunting, from a twelfth-century manuscript. (Ms. Hunter 229)

BELOW A Saxon hunting with a sling, from a twelfth-century manuscript.

RIGHT Harold, carrying his hawk and accompanied by his hounds, riding down to the coast before sailing to Normandy.

FAR RIGHT A twelfth-century carving of a French troubadour.

RIGHT, BELOW The Normans dine after landing in England. Servants prepare the dinner, and in the centre of the table, on the left of Duke William, Bishop Odo says grace.

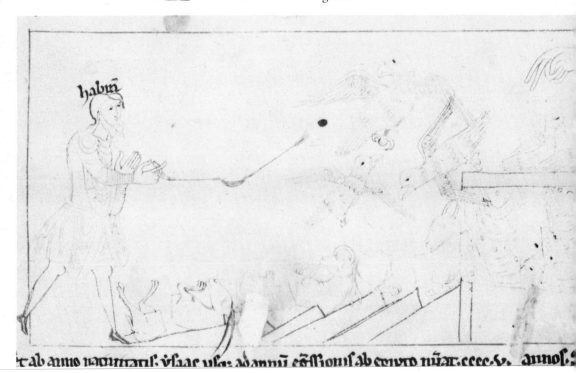

96

97

William Rufus, from a
fifteenth-century
manuscript.

nineteenth century, the passionately pro-Saxon E.A.Freeman concluded that, among other unspeakable things, William was homosexual. He never married; he had no known children; references to his mistresses are very few, although not non-existent, as Freeman suggests; and, whatever they were, his vices were enough to appal his brother Henry, who was himself a prolific fornicator. So he may have been homosexual, but these facts, combined with the rest of William's ostentatiously virile behaviour, could as easily be used to deduce that he was impotent. On such evidence as there is, the atmosphere in William's household appears to have been more like a degenerate officers' mess than a perverted brothel. It has also been suggested that William was an atheist and even that he dabbled in witchcraft. He was certainly contemptuous of religion and the church, but he once revealed a pathetic fear of God when he thought that he was dying. The anecdotes that were recorded as examples of his blasphemy amount to little more than showing off: the crude king swore like any Norman trooper and, proud of his probably undeserved reputation as a wit, amused his favourites by shocking the clergy with profanities.

Yet William had kingly qualities: he was strong-willed, he was energetic, he was sometimes shrewd, he was a capable soldier and he was recklessly courageous. These were qualities which even his critics admitted, and they might well have eclipsed his private vices if it had not been for the baser nature that dominated his public conduct. In accordance with his chivalric pretensions, he was generous to his chosen fellows, honourable to accepted equals and magnanimous to worthy enemies, but in his dealings with his subjects or his affairs of state he was callously oppressive, boastfully unscrupulous and consistently treacherous.

Not surprisingly, Archbishop Lanfranc was reluctant to acknowledge William, but eventually he acceded to the will of his friend and, on 26 September, he crowned the new king at Westminster. Following his lead, the barons swore their allegiance. The elective monarchy of England had become hereditary, and the recognition of the king's chosen heir had passed from his council to his archbishop.

After the coronation William went to the royal treasury at

The great scholar and statesman, Archbishop Lanfranc, from the opening of his *De Corpore et Sanguine Domini*, which he wrote in defence of the doctrine of transubstantiation. (Ms. Bodley 569, f. 1)

OPPOSITE Durham cathedral, looking into the nave from the south triforium.

Winchester, where he distributed gifts to the church and the poor in accordance with his father's will, and on his return to London for Christmas he reinstated his uncle Odo as Earl of Kent. It was his first mistake. Odo had long been jealous of Lanfranc. He aspired at least to the position of the king's new chief minister, William of Saint Calais, Bishop of Durham, and, like many other barons, saw more hope for the fulfilment of his ambitions in the government of an easily manipulated Robert. Within weeks of his reinstatement, Odo was planning a rebellion in Robert's favour. Among his fellow-conspirators there were a few who honestly believed that as the eldest son Robert was the rightful king, but there were more who sought their own ends, and there were many who envied the chaos of Normandy, where barons built castles without licences and conducted their private wars unimpeded.

In February 1088, knowing that a rebellion was imminent, William of Saint Calais withdrew from court, intending to remain aloof until the outcome was certain, but in March he found himself beleaguered in Durham Castle while the angry

LEFT The city of Durham, still dominated by the great cathedral and the castle, which has largely been rebuilt and extended since the Norman period.

BELOW Pevensey, the first English castle built by William the Conqueror, who began it soon after he landed, using the ruins of a Roman fort.

king's men seized his land. Then, at Easter, the rebels struck simultaneously throughout the kingdom. Their object was to create confusion and distract the King's limited military resources while Duke Robert landed in the south-east with an army from Normandy. Several royal castles were captured, including one of the strongest, at Bristol, which fell to Bishop Geoffrey of Coutances and his nephew Robert de Mowbray, Earl of Northumberland. Outside Worcester a dangerous alliance, which included Roger Montgomery, Earl of Shrewsbury, Count William of Eu and Roger de Lacy, was splendidly routed by the fyrd and a few loyal Normans under the gallant old Saxon bishop. But the risings elsewhere were ignored, and William, believing that the rebellions would fall with their leaders, concentrated his attentions on the south-east. His uncle Odo had garrisoned Rochester with a Norman detachment that had slipped into the kingdom under the Earl of Shrewsbury's son, Robert of Bellême; his other uncle, Count Robert of Mortain, held Pevensey; and the Earl of Tunbridge, Gilbert de Clare, had closed his town's gates and professed himself to be their ally.

With little reliable Norman support, William turned to the English. 'He prayed their help, and promised them the best laws that ever were in this land, and that he would forbid all unjust taxation and give them back their woods and their hunting.' The soldiers of the south-eastern fyrd believed him; eager to fight and die if need be, they followed their new king and his archbishop south from London. Since they had too few men to put a force into the field, the south-eastern rebels were compelled to remain on the defensive until the arrival of Duke Robert's Norman army, and the reliance on Duke Robert had been the flaw in their initial plan. When Tunbridge fell after only two days, Odo left his garrison and withdrew to join his brother in Pevensey. Marching after him, William invested the landward sides of the town with his army and summoned ships to blockade the harbour. The vital port withstood his assaults, but the ships that brought the Norman vanguard to relieve it were intercepted and sunk by the English fleet off Hastings. The supplies ran out and, after six weeks, Odo negotiated a surrender.

As one of the terms of the surrender Odo agreed to order the

Norman garrison to surrender Rochester as well. When he rode up to the gate, however, he allowed them to capture him instead, and William reassembled his fyrd for another siege. Still waiting for the arrival of the Duke of Normandy's army, Odo clung desperately to his last stronghold, but since the loss of the Norman vanguard he had been waiting in vain. Discouraged by an initial setback, Duke Robert had abandoned his English supporters. When an epidemic prostrated the garrison, Odo again negotiated a surrender, and with it, as William had expected, the rebellions elsewhere collapsed. Although the English clamoured for blood, the Normans in William's army urged him to be magnanimous and, flushed with victory, he was in a mood to be persuaded. He exiled the lesser rebels, he exiled Odo and, after a trial for treason, he exiled William of Saint Calais, but, perhaps because they had been loyal to his father, he pardoned the rest of the rebel leaders – it was his second mistake.

Soon after this, William lost the sympathy and support of Lanfranc. He kept none of the pledges that he had given to the fyrd, and when the archbishop reproached him for it he only answered as he was often to answer: 'Who can fulfil all that he promises?' But Lanfranc was old; within a year, on 24 May 1089, he died, and there was no one left to act as the King's conscience. Thereafter William turned more and more to the advice of men like Ranulf, an ingratiating official of the treasury, who had been nicknamed 'Flambard' for his burning ambition. As illiterate and unscrupulous as the king, Ranulf Flambard possessed a simple and shameless talent for raising money. On Lanfranc's death William left the see of Canterbury vacant and appointed Ranulf to manage the archbisopric's estates for the benefit of the crown. As other bishops and abbots died, the custom spread. The incomes from the estates of the vacant sees and abbacies were paid into the treasury; and when the need for immediate cash grew greater, some of the land was sold to laymen, and the few favourites who were actually appointed to vacant benefices were expected to pay for them. The estates of the laity were no less exploited: the inconvenient restraints of feudal customs and contracts were ignored; huge fines were imposed for the smallest offences; the estates of all but the most dangerously powerful barons were treated as though

105

they were not hereditary, and the heirs had to buy their inheritances. Even in the collection of the ordinary annual taxes Ranulf Flambard was so zealous that he was said to have trebled their yield.

With the revenues raised by Ranulf Flambard, William was soon ready to retaliate against Robert, and at a council in Winchester at Easter 1090 he planned an invasion of Normandy. Robert was growing weaker and poorer by the day: he had already lost control of Maine, and the province of the Cotentin, which produced about a third of the duchy's income, had been sold or mortgaged to Henry for most of his legacy. But King Philip of France was willing to protect his weak neighbour and vassal against a potentially strong one, and the Norman barons were more than ready to defend the duke who could not restrain their private wars. The only Normans who welcomed the prospect of William's rule were the peasants, who suffered in the anarchy, and the merchants, whose trade was disrupted by it.

William might have had more powerful allies if he had been capable of keeping his word. Soon after the defeat of Odo's rebellion, his brother Henry and Robert of Bellême had visited him in London, where he had welcomed and pardoned Robert of Bellême and confirmed Henry in the inheritance of his mother's English estates. On their return to Normandy, Duke Robert had imprisoned them as traitors, and only released them to halt the rebellions of their vassals and Robert of Bellême's family. But, by the time William's army invaded in the summer of 1090, he had lost their support by giving Henry's estates to another baron. It was to be a feature of William's reign that brothers and barons changed sides as often as the king broke his promises.

While William captured castles and bribed the king of France to keep out, the citizens of Rouen, led by a rich merchant called Conan, negotiated with him for the surrender of the city, and from the safety of Rouen castle Duke Robert negotiated for the support of Henry and Robert of Bellême. At the very moment

The ruins of the Chateau-sur-Epte, which was built by William Rufus.

The seal of William Rufus on a writ granting estates in East Anglia to Battle Abbey.

when Conan was opening Rouen's western gate to William's soldiers, Henry and Robert of Bellême were leading their army in through the gate in the south. In a running battle through the streets the English and their allies were defeated, and afterwards Henry summoned the captured Conan to the castle tower and pushed him to his death. But in February 1091 William returned, so heavily reinforced with the wealth and manpower of England that Duke Robert could do nothing but sue for peace. He gave William Fécamp and allowed him to retain the estates that he had captured, and, in return, William promised to pardon all exiles except Odo and to help Robert recover the land that he had lost elsewhere. The agreement was more to Robert's advantage than he could have hoped, and in his unjustified interpretation of it he proved every bit as capable of treachery and ingratitude as William. Instead of leading their armies against Maine, as might have been expected, Robert and William attacked and overwhelmed their younger brother's province of the Cotentin. Robert recovered his rich land, William was rewarded with Cherbourg and Mont St Michel, and Henry was reduced to landless penury.

There was no reason why Henry should ever trust either of his brothers again, but, without any practical alternative, he allowed himself to be reconciled with them and agreed to join them in a campaign which William was planning against Scotland. A lesser and unnecessary term of William's agreement with Robert had been the expulsion of Edgar the Atheling, who had been living at the Norman court as one of Robert's closest companions. Edgar had gone to Scotland, and, while Robert and William were attacking Henry, King Malcolm had once again invaded England on his behalf, and then withdrawn at the appearance of the northern fyrd. To keep his brothers from plotting behind his back, William persuaded them to join him in his retaliation.

In August the Conqueror's three sons returned to England, and in the autumn they marched north as merrily as if they were on a crusade. By the time they reached Scotland, however, their soldiers were exhausted and short of supplies, and their supporting fleet had been wrecked in a storm. A peace was negotiated by the two friends, Robert and Edgar, and William sensibly agreed to allow Edgar to return to Normandy. But it was not long before William was breaking his promises. At the end of the year Robert left England, despairing that William would ever help him in the recovery of Maine; and in 1092 William invaded western Cumberland and Westmoreland, which still belonged to Scotland, garrisoned Carlisle and colonized the whole area with English settlers.

After the conquest of the north-east there was a brief respite in the king's career of treachery. At the beginning of February 1093, at Alveston in Gloucestershire, he became so sick that he thought he was dying. At that moment at least he had enough conscience to fear for his soul, and for the first time he listened to his clergy. Since the death of Lanfranc they had been without a spokesman and leader in Canterbury, and they had helplessly suffered the erosion of their authority and the rape of their revenues by Ranulf Flambard. In desperation they had invited Lanfranc's pupil Anselm of Aosta to come over from Bec, and they had cautiously brought him to the king's attention as a worthy successor. Too fearful to make direct demands, they had once asked only for permission to pray that the king might be guided to appoint an archbishop, to which William had answered: 'Pray as you please: I shall do as I please.' But now the king seemed ready to make amends. He agreed to end oppression, to forgive all debts and to restore the abandoned laws and make the new ones that he had previously promised. He issued a writ releasing the men whom he had wrongfully imprisoned, he filled the vacant see of Lincoln – although he managed to give it to his chaplain and councillor Robert Bloet – and, to the exultant relief of all, he appointed the reluctant Anselm as Archbishop of Canterbury. Almost immediately, William recovered. He could not revoke his writs or his appointments, but he felt no need to fulfil his promises. Oppression continued, and the king was himself again.

At the end of August William summoned King Malcolm to his court at Gloucester and then refused to see him. Infuriated, and unable to protest about the invasion of the north-east, Malcolm returned to Scotland and at the end of the year invaded England. On the banks of the river Alne, at a place now known as Malcolm's Cross, he was defeated and killed by Robert de Mowbray. Queen Margaret, who was already dying, did not long outlive him; on the day of her funeral Malcolm's brother Donaldbane entered Edinburgh with an army of Scots and Norwegians to seize the throne, and her five surviving sons fled. Malcolm's eldest son Duncan, who had been born before his marriage to Margaret, was still a hostage at the English court, and at once William allowed him to levy soldiers in return for his homage. Duncan marched north and was briefly successful, but in the end he was killed. Donaldbane recovered the throne, and William's interference had earned him a dangerous enemy. During the next three years, while William's attentions were diverted by war in Normandy and another baronial rebellion, it was fortunate that Donaldbane did not invade England.

At Christmas 1093 William received ambassadors from Robert demanding compensation for his failure to support him in the recovery of Maine, and threatening war if he refused. Naturally, William chose war. In March 1094, after attending the consecration of Battle Abbey, out of respect for his father rather than piety, he sailed with his English army from Hastings. Prolonged and inconclusive fighting continued until 1095, when William again bribed King Philip, whose soldiers this time had actually been fighting beside Robert's, and won the support of Henry, who had been living in unprincely privation with a small retinue at the border castle of Domfront. But William could not continue to fight with any certainty of success. He had been spending money faster than Ranulf Flambard could raise it, and in their efforts they resorted to a ruse which utterly typified the methods of the Red King and his treasurer. On William's orders, a new fyrd was summoned to reinforce the army in Normandy. Before leaving his shire, each of the 20,000 English soldiers was provided with ten shillings to cover his expenses; but when they assembled at Hastings, Ranulf Flambard ordered them to hand it over and then, dismissing them, sent their 10,000 pounds to Normandy, where it was used in part to swell the French king's bribe, and in part to pay Normans to continue fighting under Henry while William went home.

Soon after his return, William's uneasy relationship with Anselm erupted into open conflict. It was two years since Anselm had been appointed to the see of Canterbury, and if he did not soon receive his *pallium* from a pope he could not honourably retain the office. His loyalty lay with Pope Urban II in Rome, rather than the anti-Pope Clement III, but William, who had been careful to commit himself to neither, refused him permission to leave the kingdom and warned him that he could be guilty of treason if he did. Anselm maintained adamantly that his spiritual allegiance was beyond the jurisdiction of a temporal power, to which William countered with some justification that in England no pope could be recognized without the king's consent.

Hoping that treasonable defiance might be accepted as grounds for dismissing his archbishop, William submitted his case to a council at Rockingham. Unexpectedly, however, the barons at the council, who resented William's attempts to blackmail them, found no fault with Anselm. 'By God's face,' yelled William, 'if you will not condemn him as I wish, I will condemn you', and in desperation he resorted to secret negotiations with Urban, naively offering recognition in return for a judgement in his favour. The Pope dispatched a legate and, on his arrival, the legate argued reasonably that he had no jurisdiction to judge Anselm until his master's authority had been recognized within the kingdom. Then, when William had eagerly sworn his allegiance, the legate announced that the Holy Father would never consent to the dismissal of his loyal archbishop.

Infuriated, thwarted and tricked into recognizing a pope by his own deceit, William could do nothing but accept a hollow reconciliation with Anselm. No matter how it had been obtained, a vow of allegiance to a pope was so sacred in the eyes of Christendom that, even to William, it was not worth the risk to renounce it. For the time being he could do no more than subject Anselm to his usual petty feudal persecution, but in 1097 he allowed him to leave the kingdom, repossessing the lands of Canterbury as soon as he had gone, and Anselm remained in exile for the rest of the reign.

While William was humiliating himself in his feud with his Archbishop, a second rebellion was being planned by the very barons he had pardoned in 1088. Contemptuous of Robert's indolence, they chose to replace their king with Stephen of Aumale, the son of the Conqueror's niece and Count Odo of Champagne. William suspected a conspiracy and, when the Earl of Northumberland, Robert de Mowbray, refused to appear at court to answer a charge of plundering four Norwegian ships, he guessed rightly that the earl was one of the leaders. Raising an army, he marched north, ostensibly to punish Earl Robert for his crime and disobedience, and on the way the entire plot was revealed to him. In return for a pardon, a pessimistic and repentant Gilbert de Clare betrayed the names of his fellow-conspirators and warned the king that he was marching into an ambush. William changed his route, and when he reached Northumberland in safety, Earl Robert was abandoned by his frustrated allies. After three months of siege warfare, from which William was briefly diverted by an unconnected rising in Wales, the rebel castles fell and Earl Robert was imprisoned for life. In January 1096, at a council in Salisbury, William turned with varying degrees of vengeance on the other conspirators. Most of the leaders were heavily fined, but the lesser knights were hanged or blinded, Roger de

Lacy and Count Odo of Champagne were deprived of their English estates, and the unfortunate William of Eu, apparently on the insistence of his wife's family, was blinded and castrated.

During the first eight years of his reign, most of William's schemes had been frustrated and his achievements had amounted to little more than a few small conquests and the retention of his throne. In 1096 the tide turned unexpectedly. Without a drop of bloodshed, William temporarily became master of Normandy. Somehow, against all common sense, Duke Robert was persuaded to go on a crusade and, since he could not afford to pay for it, he offered to mortgage Normandy to William. By doubling the Danegeld and forcing some churches to sell their relics, Ranulf Flambard raised the stipulated 10,000 marks. William took it to Normandy and, after the brothers had agreed that if either died childless the other would be his heir, Robert set out for the Holy Land.

No longer threatened by rebellion at home, and relieved of the expenses of his wars with Robert, William was free to turn his attentions to Scotland and Wales and, as ruler of Normandy, he at last became interested in the recovery of Maine. In 1097 he again allowed a pretender to the Scots' throne to levy English and Norman soldiers in return for his homage. This time it was Edgar, one of the sons of Malcolm and Margaret, and when he marched north his uncle, Edgar the Atheling, went with him as an adviser. The defeated Donaldbane was blinded and imprisoned. After Edgar's coronation, Edgar the Atheling left Edinburgh to join Duke Robert on his crusade, and for the rest of his life the new king of Scots was a loyal vassal of the English throne.

William was less successful with Wales. Although his border barons extended their domains, their outposts often fell to retaliatory raids; the three expeditions which William led himself failed ignominiously when the Welsh withdrew to the mountains where Norman cavalry was useless; and, in Anglesey in 1098, a baronial invasion ended in the disastrous defeat and death of Hugh Montgomery, who had succeeded his father as Earl of Shrewsbury. But at least the Welsh were contained. William sold the earldom of Shrewsbury to Hugh's brother, Robert of Bellême, and in him he found a man who could control the Welsh marches as no one else would have done.

A European soldier in Jerusalem, c. 1109.

113

ABOVE AND RIGHT Anselm, saint, scholar and
archbishop of Canterbury, from a late
twelfth-century manuscript. (Ms. Bodley
271, ff. iiv and 43v)

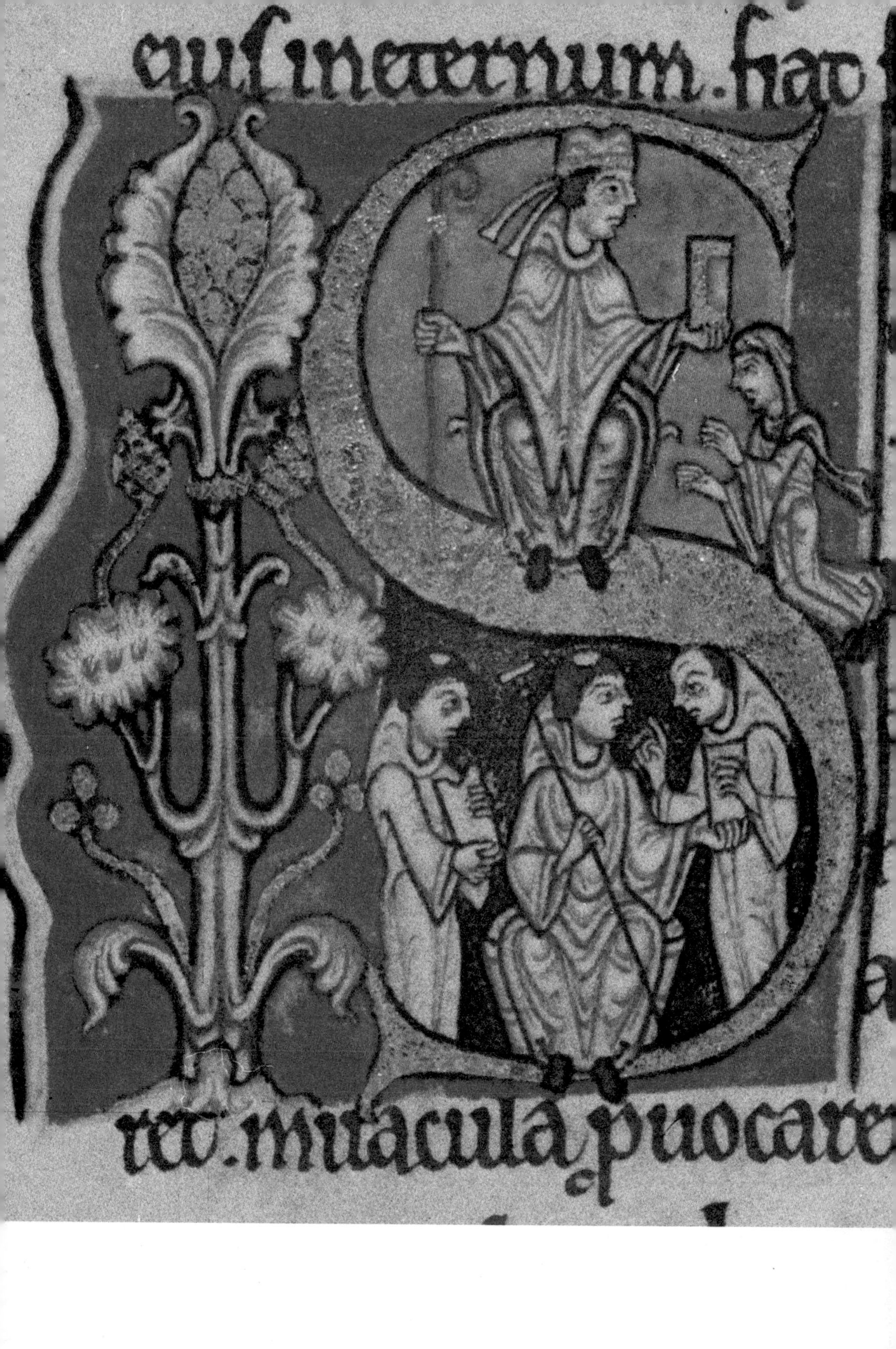

Robert of Bellême was an experienced and capable soldier, and an accomplished military architect, but behind his courteous manner lay the most vicious, wicked and calculatingly cruel Norman baron that ever set foot in England. He invented new forms of torture for his prisoners and he was so utterly devoid of compassion that he once pushed out the eyes of his own godson because the boy's father had irritated him. Hemmed in by his new castles and his rapacious soldiers, the Welsh could not hope to regain the land that they had lost and, to retain what remained, a few of them became his allies.

Meanwhile, William's armies were fighting on the borders of Normandy. In November 1097 he led one army into the Vexin and, in January 1098, before the earldom of Shrewsbury fell vacant, he sent another into Maine under Robert of Bellême. But the simultaneous campaigns stretched William's depleted resources beyond even Ranulf Flambard's limits, and neither was ultimately successful. Although Le Mans was taken in 1098, William's soldiers were unable to hold it and he had to return from England to recapture it in 1099. In the early summer of 1100, however, the Duke of Aquitaine, who was William's ally, decided that he too would go on a crusade and, like Robert, he offered to mortgage his duchy to William. William was overjoyed. He prepared grandiose schemes for the conquest of all western France, he ordered the building of a new fleet and he assembled a new army, with which he intended to begin by holding Normandy against Robert when he returned from the Holy Land. On the first of August, while he was shooting deer in the New Forest, one of his party asked him where he intended to keep Christmas, and he answered proudly that he would keep it in Poitiers. But he was never again to keep Christmas anywhere. During the hunt on the following evening, William Rufus fell dead, with an arrow in his heart.

William's brother Henry was among the seven lords who accompanied him on that fatal evening. When they were informed that the king had been shot by accident, Henry left at once, rode full gallop to Winchester and seized the Treasury. Early next morning the King's body, which had apparently been abandoned by the rest of the party, was brought to Winchester in a charcoal-burner's cart by a group of peasants and hastily buried beneath the cathedral tower. When the tower fell down seven years later, it was said to be because the body beneath was unworthy of its resting-place. After the burial Henry held an impromptu council, at which he was elected king, and then rode with an entourage to London, which he reached that evening. On the following day he held a court, to which he summoned the Bishop of London, and on the day after that, Sunday 5 August, in the absence of the Archbishop of Canterbury, the Bishop of London crowned him in Westminster Abbey.

At the time nobody said that King William's death was anything other than an accident, although some added that it was caused by the merciful intervention of God. Nevertheless there is a great deal of circumstantial evidence that suggests a conspiracy to murder. In the first place, Henry's only real chance of ascending the throne of England lay in William's dying before the end of August. By then William's chosen heir, Robert, who would be expected to succeed without much opposition, was due to return from his crusade and, since it had just been learned that he was bringing a wife with him, it was likely that he in turn would be succeeded by a legitimate son. Henry had a motive for murder: in the king's party, let alone the hunt servants, he had potential accomplices; in the hunt he had the ideal opportunity for making murder look like an accident; and as the man who pushed Conan to his death and was later to prove the cruellest of the Norman kings, even to his family, he was at least capable of contemplating it. In no more than seventy crucial hours between William's death and Henry's coronation, Henry wasted no time and made no mistakes. His actions were so cool, synchronized and constructive that it is difficult to believe they were not planned in advance.

On the evening of his death, according to William of Malmesbury and Orderic Vitalis, King William stood up from behind his cover and shot at a stag, which ran away wounded. Then, as a second stag ran past him, Walter Tirel, the Lord of Poix in Normandy, who was apparently an expert shot, loosed an arrow which narrowly missed the second stag and flew on to kill the king. It follows from this story that the stag had run into the line of archers, and that the best shot so far forgot himself as to loose an arrow knowing that another member of the party

King William II and King
Henry I, sons of the
Conqueror, from a
fourteenth-century
manuscript.

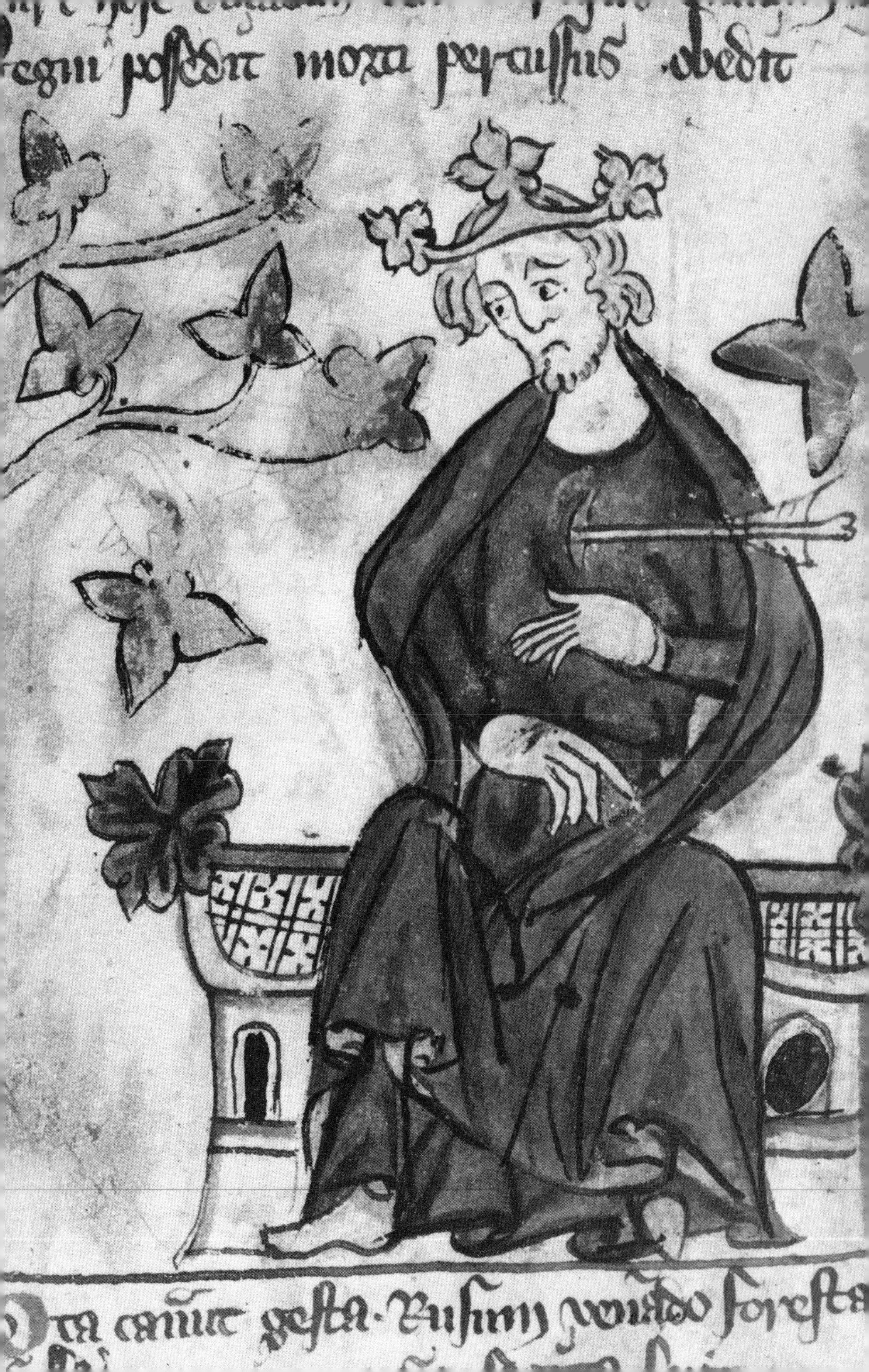

The death of William
Rufus in the New Forest,
from a fourteenth-century
manuscript.

William Rufus is killed in
the New Forest, and the
news is brought to his
brother, Henry I, from a
fifteenth-century
manuscript. 122

would be in its path if he missed. Furthermore, the arrow struck the king in the heart – a very unlucky place to be hit by accident. The other chroniclers do not entirely agree with this story: although he repeated it, Geoffrey Gaimar added suspiciously that it was the other archers who said that the arrow came from Tirel's bow, and that it seemed likely because he promptly fled; the *Anglo-Saxon Chronicle* simply recorded that the king was shot by one of his men; John of Salisbury said that William shot himself; Eadmer said that it was uncertain whether the arrow came from another archer or whether the king fell on it; and Gerald of Wales attributed the shot to a man whom he called 'Ranulf de Aquis'. There is little doubt, however, that on the evening of the hunt Tirel was held responsible. Understandably fearing a reprisal, he fled to the coast that night and sailed for Normandy the following morning. However, for the rest of his life, and even on his deathbed, he adamantly maintained that he had not shot the arrow, and that he was not even in the same part of the forest as the king.

If Tirel was lying, he was either an assassin or else he was so ashamed of the accident and afraid of a reprisal that he carried the lie to his grave. But if Tirel was telling the truth, it is possible that, whether the king's death was an accident or not, Tirel was an innocent scapegoat, who was accused and then persuaded to fly in order to draw the blame away from somebody else. Whatever the truth, his speed of action was as suspicious as Henry's. He was a stranger to Hampshire, he could not possibly have reached the coast as quickly as he did without at least a guide, and, unless he was carrying enough money to pay for his ship, that ship was laid on in advance. He must have received help – and there were two men who may well have provided it.

By his marriage to Alice de Clare, Walter Tirel had allied himself to two great families: Alice's uncle, William Giffard, was King William's chancellor, her sister was married to one of Henry's best friends, and the eldest of her three brothers was the rebel turncoat Gilbert de Clare, Earl of Tunbridge. On the evening of the king's death Gilbert and his brother Roger were with their brother-in-law Walter Tirel in the royal hunting-party. They accompanied Henry on his gallop to Winchester, where, amongst other courtiers, they met their uncle, William

Giffard, and next day they rode on with Henry to London. On the morning after William's death, Henry appointed William Giffard to the vacant see of Winchester, the richest in England; shortly after his coronation he appointed Alice Tirel's third brother Richard, who was a monk at Bec, to the vacant abbacy of Ely; and ten years later he granted the lordship of the shire of Cardigan to her eldest brother Gilbert. The house of Clare was a staunch ally of Henry's, and it is not surprising that he favoured its members. But it is at least a strange coincidence that Gilbert de Clare, who had twice plotted against William, who was present at his death, whose family gained by it and who supported Henry in the critical hours that followed it, was also the brother-in-law of the man who was blamed for it.

Walter Tirel received neither reward nor retribution, and the honours received by his powerful kinsmen were lost among the many that Henry distributed. William's supporters, and even his chosen heir Robert, were convinced by the story of the accident, and there was no need for an inquiry. If there had been an inquiry, the evidence of witnesses might well have corroborated that story, but today, without their evidence, a verdict of accidental death is very hard to accept.

Late Norman arches in the nave of the cathedral at Ely.

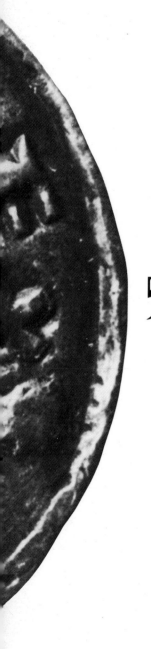

5 'The Lion of Justice'

HENRY I WAS NEARLY thirty-two years old when he came to the throne of England. Like his brothers he was heavily built, but his eyes were softer than theirs and his temperament was deceptively more placid. As his mother's favourite he had received a better education than her other children, and he was proud of his greatly exaggerated reputation for scholarship. His only cultural pretension, however, was the curiosity that led him to maintain a magnificent menagerie at Woodstock, and the suggestions that he had translated some of the classics were no more than flattering rumours. Nevertheless, he had some understanding of Latin, and he learned to speak enough English to argue Saxon law in it.

Since the death of his father he had suffered or prospered at the whim of his contentious brothers, and while he consoled himself with women who might have been better described as strumpets than mistresses, his heart had hardened. He was only capable of apparent generosity when he regarded his gift as an investment. Although he was genuinely fond of his legitimate children, his nephews of the house of Blois and a few favourite bastards, he was callously indifferent towards the rest of his progeny. Where the other Norman kings had been merciless, Henry was gratuitously cruel. He was at least as ruthless as his father, at times as untrustworthy as his brothers, and in avarice surpassed them all. But as an administrator, a diplomat and a soldier he was the most versatile and accomplished of the Conqueror's sons.

Unlike his older brothers, Henry had been born in England; and it was on this that he based his claim to the throne. According to one custom prevalent in parts of feudal Europe, a son who had been born while his father was a reigning king was said to have been 'born in the purple', and to hold precedence over the sons who had been born before their father's elevation. Henry did not claim therefore that he was the rightful heir to his brother; he claimed that he was the rightful heir to his father and that his brother had been a usurper. It was an argument which the English were soon ready to accept, and most of the Normans, who were not, could not oppose it until their better candidate returned from the Crusades. When he did, Henry was as beset by barons and his brother as William Rufus had been.

Immediately after his coronation Henry issued a solemn

PREVIOUS PAGES A silver penny, minted in the reign of Henry I. Pennies, or sterlings, were first issued in the last quarter of the eighth century by the Saxons, who minted 240 from each pound of silver. Under the Normans, the obsolete Saxon shilling, which had once been worth about five pence, was reintroduced, not as a coin but as an accounting measure denoting twelve pence.

OPPOSITE King Henry I, The Lion of Justice, from an early fifteenth-century manuscript.

charter of liberties and sent copies to be read in every shire. In it he promised to abolish all the evil practices introduced by his brother, to keep good peace throughout the kingdom and to restore all the laws of his father and King Edward. In spirit his promises were little different to the promises that his brother had made to the English fyrd and at Alveston, but Henry's subsequent conduct induced the hope that this time they might be fulfilled. He imprisoned Ranulf Flambard, he wrote to Anselm inviting him to return, he began to fill the vacant bishoprics and abbeys and, above all, he married Edith, the daughter of King Malcolm and Queen Margaret.

As much as his ancestors and more than his brothers, Henry understood the political value of dynastic marriages; later in his reign they were to play a vital part in his ambitious foreign policies. Through her mother, Edith was the great-grand-daughter of King Edmund Ironside, and in the children that she would bear, the blood of the ruling houses of England, Scotland and Normandy would be united. To the haughty Normans the king's marriage to a subject Saxon princess was contemptible, and they nicknamed the royal couple 'Godric and Godgifu', but to the rejoicing English it was a symbol of Henry's unity with his people.

Edith, who took the name Matilda, had been educated in a convent, and, like many of her contemporaries, had worn a nun's habit to protect herself from becoming an unwilling bride, but Anselm had ruled that she had taken no vows which would be a bar to her marriage. She was a homely queen; in a clumsy and almost untranslatable back-handed compliment, William of Malmesbury described her as 'by no means continually despicable in appearance'. But her piety and charity won her the respect of the clergy, and armed her with the humble dignity with which she resigned herself to the slights of a promiscuous husband who acknowledged more than twenty bastards.

In September 1100 Duke Robert came home to Normandy. He had distinguished himself in the Holy Land, leading assaults on Antioch and Jerusalem, and so impressing his fellow commanders that they offered to make him Jerusalem's king. But the crusade was to be the only glorious episode in his life. By the time he returned he had already squandered his wife's rich dowry, and for ever afterwards he was as gullible and irresolute as he had been before he left. In spite of invitations from English barons, he made no effort to assert his claim to Henry's throne until, in February 1101, Ranulf Flambard escaped from prison while his guards were drunk and went to Normandy, where he persuaded Robert that the barons of England were indeed ready to support an invasion. He was not far wrong: the majority welcomed the prospect of Robert's ineffectual rule and, although only a few were prepared to fight beside him, many were merely waiting for his victory to swear their allegiance. Since the return of Anselm Henry had the support of the church, and by his marriage and his charter of liberties, which he reissued when he learned that an invasion was imminent, he had won the loyalty of the fyrd. But his reliable Norman supporters were few, and after he had been abandoned by Robert of Bellême, who was by now the most powerful baron in England, it was only through the efforts of Anselm that others did not follow the example.

On 21 July 1101, having avoided Henry's fleet with the help of English pilots, Duke Robert landed his powerful Norman army unopposed at Portsmouth. With his strength increased by a few rash barons, he marched towards London. At Alton Henry barred the road with the fyrd and the feudal levies of the loyal Normans and the church. The odds were in Robert's favour, but Henry's greatest ally was his knowledge of his brother. After preparing his fyrd to withstand the impact of a Norman cavalry charge, he rode forward to negotiate. He offered an amnesty for Robert's allies, he offered to relinquish the estates which William had given to him in Normandy, he made the usual promise to assist in the recovery of Maine and he offered to pay Robert an annuity of 3,000 marks. As his allies should by now have learned to expect, Robert readily agreed, and withdrew his army to Normandy. With the throne of England within his grasp, he had thrown it away for a few Norman promises.

Since he had promised them a pardon, Henry was devious in his retribution against the barons who had opposed or abandoned him. One by one he brought them before his council to answer trumped-up charges of crimes and feudal offences; and then he ruined them with exorbitant fines. But

The cross on the reverse of the penny, minted in the reign of Henry I.

Robert of Bellême and his two brothers hurriedly provisioned their castles, Robert bought the loyalty of his Welsh vassals with horses and grants of land, and when the king's summons came they refused to answer it. With his loyal Normans and the eager fyrd, Henry attacked. Fortunately for him, the brothers' many formidable castles were too far apart to aid each other, and Robert's most powerful vassal, Prince Jorwerth ap Bleddyn, was seduced by a counter-bribe of the principality of South Wales. Besieged, isolated, deprived of Welsh support and with no hope of help from the other apprehensive barons, the brothers surrendered. Although his Norman commanders pleaded for clemency, Henry deprived the brothers of every acre of their land in England. His victory had secured his throne, the English celebrated it in a ballad, and when Prince Jorwerth ap Bleddyn claimed his reward, Henry refused and then imprisoned him. Retiring to Normandy, Robert of Bellême established a refuge for other angry exiles, and began to wreak his vengeance on the feeble duke whom he blamed for his downfall.

Although Archbishop Anselm had supported Henry against his brother and his barons, the old conflict between the church and the crown had not been forgotten. The English king's right to invest his own bishops had only been conceded for the reign of William I, and a recent Lateran council, which Anselm had attended, had repeated the decrees against lay investitures. On his return, in obedience to these decrees, Anselm refused to pay homage to Henry for the estates of Canterbury and to recognize the new bishops whom Henry had invested. Henry was as adamant in the maintenance of his right as Anselm was in opposing it, but the argument was conducted in a far more civilized atmosphere than in the previous reign. Each respected the other's intransigence, and their relationship remained cordial. In 1103, after Pope Paschal II had refused to renew the concession that had been granted to his father, Henry suggested that Anselm should go to Rome and negotiate. Anselm agreed, but when his efforts failed he did not return to the insoluble conflict. Instead he lived in Lyons, writing friendly letters to the king, travelling north to meet him when he visited Normandy and even commanding his bishops to remain loyal to Henry until, like him, they received papal orders to the contrary.

In his absence Henry was not so honourable. He appropriated the income from the see of Canterbury to his own use, and he used Anselm's decree against married clergy as an excuse to impose heavy fines on the many who disobeyed it. In 1105, however, the Pope excommunicated Henry's bishops and warned that he would do the same to Henry if he did not submit. The king and his archbishop reopened their nego- tiations, Anselm returned to England, and in 1107 they drew up a treaty. Henry renounced the ceremonial right to invest his bishops with their ring and staff, and, with the Pope's authority, Anselm agreed that they should still pay homage to Henry for the estates that went with their offices.

The compromise was entirely in Henry's favour: as feudal lord he was still in a position to influence a bishop's election, which often took place in his own council, and the independence which the Pope had hoped to secure for his clergy was symbolic rather than practical. In Westminster, at the very council at which the terms were agreed, Anselm consecrated five bishops whom Henry had already appointed, and after Anselm's death in 1109 Henry left the see of Canterbury vacant for four years before appointing Ralph d'Escures as his successor.

Nevertheless, as time passed, the support of the papacy became a vital element in Henry's continental diplomacy, and to retain it he made limited but unwelcome concessions. In 1123 Ralph's successor, William of Corbeil, was freely elected by the conclave of Canterbury; two years later Henry allowed a papal legate to hold a council in England; and afterwards he accepted the commission of his own archbishop as a permanent legate. But he never relinquished his lucrative feudal authority and, by denying his bishops their temporal independence, he limited the influence of the reforming papacy in England and fortuitously, but more successfully than many of his contemporaries, protected his subjects and lesser clergy from what was in effect a zealous, ecclesiastical tyranny.

One of the five bishops who were consecrated at West- minster by Anselm was a once poor Norman priest called Roger, to whom Henry had given the see of Salisbury. During the reign Roger was to serve consecutively as chancellor, treasurer and justiciar in the king's council, and, since Henry

Norman Church Architecture

The Normans were the most prolific builders of their age. They manifested their wealth in the splendour of their cathedrals, churches and abbeys. All their stone buildings were larger than the Saxon buildings that they replaced, and some were larger than any in Europe. In spite of their length, however, most of the naves of Norman cathedrals were narrow. Their roofs were built of wood, so that the walls below did not have to be solid to bear the weight of stone; and in consequence their width was limited by the length of the beams. But at Durham they built the roof in stone, and for the first time rested the weight on the strength of transverse, pointed arches.

ABOVE Norman columns in York Minster.

LEFT Delicate Norman arches in the Galilee Chapel of Durham Cathedral.

RIGHT The Prior's Door at Ely Cathedral.

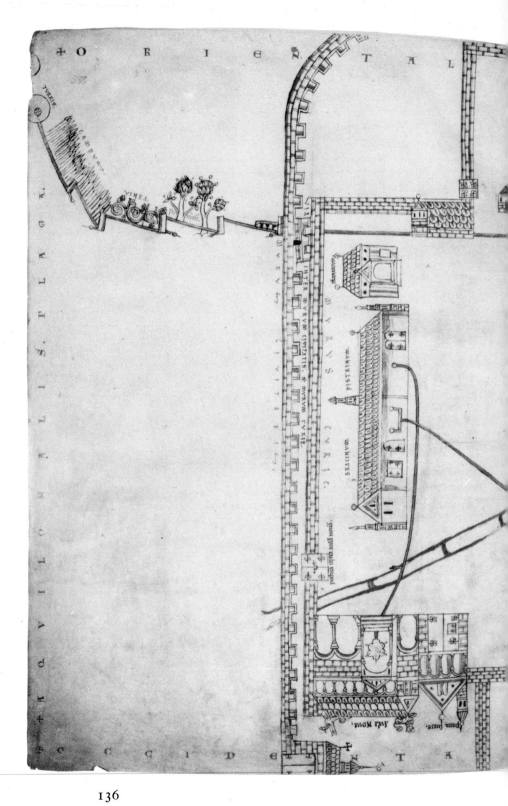

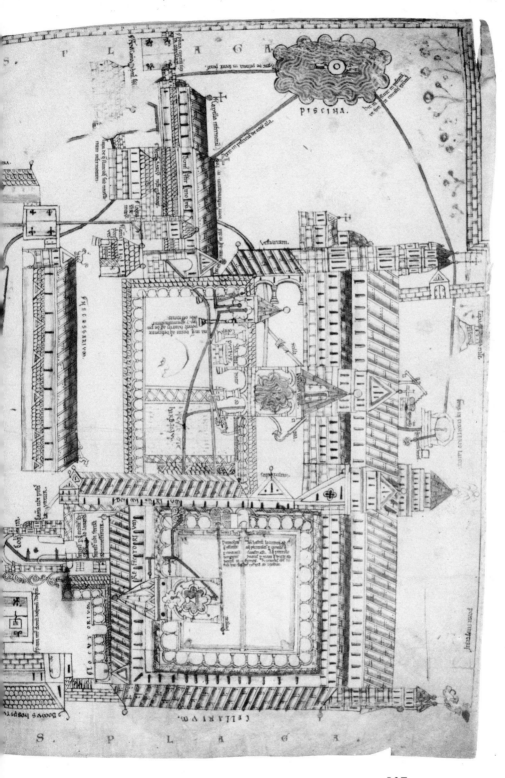

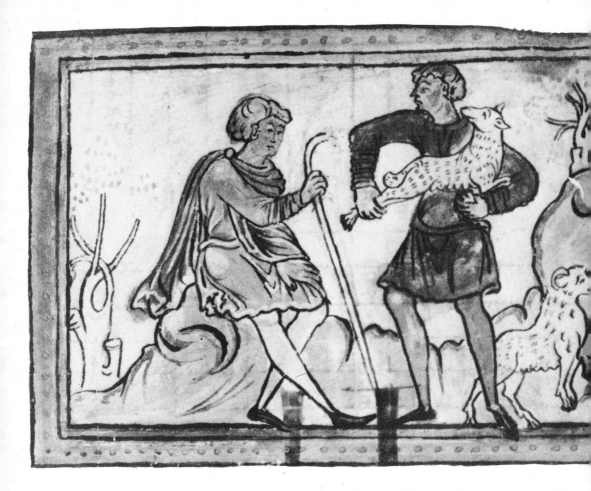

was to spend most of his time in Normandy, to serve in his absence as 'Lieutenant of the realm of England'. He was the most outstanding of the many humble men whom Henry chose on their merit and elevated not only in the church but also to the ranks of his barons. 'He raised them from the dust to do his service,' wrote Orderic Vitalis. It was with these able, reliable and ruthless men that Henry reformed and reorganized the judicial and fiscal systems that had been developed by his father and abused by his brother.

The literate king had an eye for detail and a fondness for routine, he was a good judge of his servants and above all he had a rare ability to delegate authority. But he was utterly conservative. Although his reforms were to be far-reaching in their consequences, they were neither enlightened nor radical. Like his father, Henry sought only to extend his power, regulate

PREVIOUS PAGES A plan for the projected water system at the monastery of Christ Church, Canterbury, c. 1160.

138

and control the administration of justice, and improve the collection of the revenues for which his need was insatiable.

The influence of the barons in England was growing dangerously. Intermarriage and subsequent inheritance had become liable to create combined estates that might one day be as powerful and disruptive as the feudal estates of France, and during the reign of William II the authority of the royal courts of the shires and hundreds, which had become ill-attended and irregularly held, had again been eclipsed by the private courts of the barons. To counter the growth of large estates, Henry exercised his feudal right to divide inheritances in any way that he saw fit. When, for example, Ralph de Meschin became heir to the palatine earldom of Chester, Henry only allowed him to inherit it on condition that he resigned Carlisle, which had been brought to him by his wife; and when a girl inherited

Shepherds, from an eleventh-century calendar.

Gloucester, Henry married her to his own bastard son, Robert.

To counter the growth of the private courts, Henry issued new ordinances which limited their jurisdiction. Apart from their duty to try the petty criminal offences which had been committed within their estates, the tenants–in–chief had been entitled to hear any civil suit in which the defendant was one of their own free tenants. In practice this had meant that the shire courts were deprived of most of their civil business and that defendants had the advantage of a favourable judge. But Henry enacted that a tenant-in-chief could no longer hear a civil action unless both the litigants were his own tenants and that the courts of the shires and hundreds, which would now hear most of the civil actions, should be held as regularly as they had been in the past.

From these beginnings the judicial reorganization of England grew. The number of the roving commissioners, who had already been acting as judges in the shires, was greatly increased. In most shires the important civil actions and criminal trials were saved for the visits of these itinerant justices, while in a few, permanent justices were appointed to replace the sheriff. All their courts, acting under the royal writ, became the provincial extensions of the king's council, the Curia Regis. Previously the Curia Regis had met irregularly as a law court to try suits between tenants-in-chief and to hear some appeals from the courts of the shires, but under the royal justiciar it became a permanent supreme court, and by keeping records it began to build a body of precedents upon which its future judgements might be based. Local laws still varied from shire to shire, and indeed the law of the Curia Regis itself was an amalgam of Norman and Saxon customs; nevertheless, the law which the justices applied was the law of the Curia Regis, and in every case that law held sway over the law of the shire. As time passed, local traditions lost their validity and, in the recorded judgements and precedents of the Curia Regis and its itinerant justices, the seeds of a universal English common law began to germinate.

Under the direction of Bishop Roger of Salisbury a new court was instituted to assess and collect the royal revenues. It was composed of all the leading members of the Curia Regis, and twice a year, at Easter and Michaelmas, all the sheriffs, who

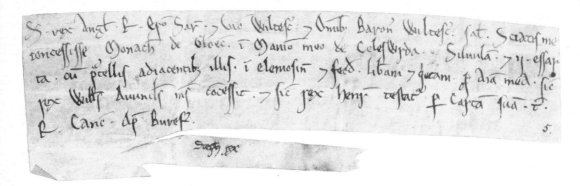

A writ to Roger, Bishop of Salisbury, and others, granting land in Celeword (Colesword) to the monks of Gloucester. (Ms. Ch. Gloucs 5, No. 5)

were responsible for the collection of the revenues in their shires, were required to appear before it in Winchester to render their accounts. Since most of the sheriffs were illiterate, the sums were calculated with counters on a large chequered cloth, which covered the table in front of the king's councillors, and it was from this cloth that the new court took its name – the Court of the Exchequer.

The sheriffs paid a fixed sum for their right to 'farm' the royal rents, and anything that they made on top of that was their own business. However, they were required to account in detail for taxes, feudal dues and the fines imposed by their courts. At Winchester they handed over their takings in the Chamber of Receipt, where, since the kingdom was full of fraudulent moneyers, the coins were assayed before being counted. Then, in the inner Chamber of Account, they made their statements of receipts and expenses before the barons of the Exchequer. At Easter, each sheriff paid as much as he had collected so far and in recognition received a tally, which was made from one half of a piece of wood that had been cut in a zig-zag down the middle, and on which each notch denoted a sum. At Michaelmas, on the production of the rest of his debt and a 'tally' which matched the half that had been kept by the Exchequer, the sheriff was acquitted. If he failed in his obligation, his deficit was recorded with the rest of the court's proceedings on the Great Roll of the Pipe, and then added to his liability in the following year; and if he was persistently in arrears, he could be fined or even imprisoned.

It was only the records of the Pipe Roll and the chambers of Receipt and Account that differentiated the proceedings of the Court of Exchequer from the other proceedings of the Curia

Regis. Although the Curia Regis was primarily composed of all the lay and ecclesiastical tenants-in-chief, the business of government was conducted by an inner circle of the king's appointed ministers and chosen councillors, and apart from the individual responsibilities of certain ministers – such as the justiciar and the treasurer – there were no separate spheres of authority. The Curia Regis made no distinction between its administrative, legislative, judicial and fiscal functions, and since they were all performed by the same men there was no need for it. As barons of the exchequer the king's councillors collected fines that they had imposed in their judicial capacity as barons of the Curia Regis, and under the justiciar they punished sheriffs whom they found to be in default under the treasurer. In time the larger body of the Curia Regis was to evolve into a Parliament, and the inner circle was to divide into the Privy Council and the King's Bench. But, from its inception, the Exchequer, with its separate chambers and records, was the first English department of government to acquire a limited identity of its own.

In the execution of Henry's judicial and fiscal reforms the charter of liberties was forgotten, and the immediate

Thirteenth-century tallies from the Court of the Exchequer. The nature of the accounts and the names of the men who paid them are written on the side, and the amounts are recorded in notches. The small notches on the two tallies above record sums in shillings and pence; the larger notches below record pounds in thousands and scores.

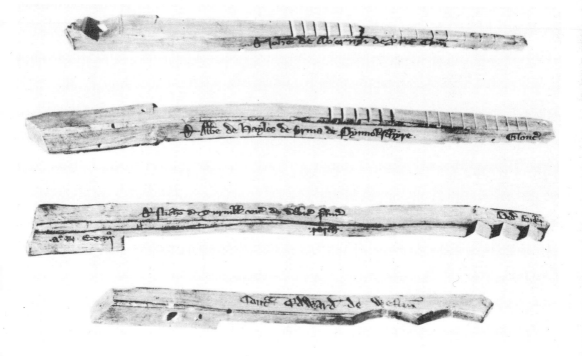

consequence was oppression. Many of the rights which he had promised to abandon were retained to meet the expenses of his increased bureaucracy and his wars. He had promised to uphold the laws of King Edward and his father, but the laws of King Edward were overridden by the new supremacy of the Curia Regis, and the death penalty for crimes against property, which William the Conqueror had commuted to mutilation, was restored. The judgements of the Curia Regis and its justices were harsh and excessive. For some crimes, fines were imposed in addition to damages and even mutilation, and it was not until late in his reign that Henry saw the advantage of fines over physical punishment.

The forest laws were enforced more severely than ever. After an inquest into the English mints, more than ninety moneyers were mutilated for debasing the coinage, and in Leicestershire an unprecedented forty-four thieves were hanged in a single session by one of the itinerant justices whom Henry had 'raised from the dust'. Fugitives from justice resorted widely to the privilege of sanctuary, whereby they were allowed to take refuge in a churchyard for up to forty days, and the clergy were so outraged by the brutality of the king's punishments that they defended the privilege fiercely. Yet, unlike the oppressions under William Rufus, the cruelty of Henry's courts and the exactions of his Exchequer were conducted within the letter of the law. Although his English subjects suffered and complained, the law was the same for them as it was for the Normans, and their limited freedom was protected by the authority of the Curia Regis and by the restriction of baronial power.

'If a lord slay his blameless villein', read the laws of King Henry, 'let him pay the compensation to his kindred; for the man was a serf to serve and not to be slain.' By the end of his reign, grudgingly and with little affection, the English had begun to recognize Henry as 'The Lion of Justice'. 'Good man he was,' wrote the Peterborough chronicler, 'and there was great awe of him. In his day no man dared harm another.'

OPPOSITE A section of the Pipe Roll for the year 1130, recording the taxes that the sheriffs had collected for the Exchequer and the amounts that were still outstanding.

6 'The Revenge for Hastings'

THE PEACE WHICH had been concluded between King Henry and Duke Robert at Alton in 1101 did not last. Henry had no intention of keeping his promises for longer than necessary. In spite of the agreed amnesty, Robert's supporters were being fined or exiled, and in 1103, when Robert came to England to plead on behalf of one of them in person, he was tricked into parting with his precious annuity. One of Henry's councillors frightened him with a friendly warning that the king intended to imprison him for encouraging another rebellion, and then persuaded him to ensure his safety by surrendering his annuity as a present for Queen Matilda. But although the exile of potential enemies was increasing Henry's control over England, it was also creating a powerful opposition in Normandy, where many of them owned estates which were large enough to provide considerable military retinues. Under the leadership of Robert of Bellême they were systematically driving Henry's friends and vassals out of the duchy; and when Henry complained that his brother had come to terms with Robert of Bellême, the duke replied with disarming honesty that he had been powerless to do anything else.

In 1104 Robert of Bellême's forces were almost doubled by the arrival of Henry's cousin, Count William of Mortain. William had supported Duke Robert's invasion of England and had yet to suffer for it when he claimed the right to inherit his uncle Odo's earldom of Kent. In accordance with his open opposition to combined estates, Henry forbade the inheritance, on the grounds that William was already Earl of Cornwall; and in accordance with his covert campaign to ruin Duke Robert's supporters, he tried him for treason and sent him into exile.

On reaching Normandy, William released his pent-up fury by joining in the attacks against some of the castles which were held by barons who also owned estates in England. To reassure these barons of his support, and to encourage them to rally to each others' defence, Henry followed with his fleet. When he met his brother, he subjected him to a devastating, self-righteous lecture on the incompetence of his government, and made such threatening protests about his continued tolerance of Robert of Bellême that Duke Robert gave him the county of Evreux in a grovelling attempt to placate him. But the gift of a

PREVIOUS PAGES The Norman keep and inner bailey of Porchester Castle, thought to date from the reign of Henry I, c. 1120.

county neither satisfied Henry nor solved the problem. The refuges of Bellême and Mortain were now dangerous bases for an English rebellion; since Robert was powerless, the only certain solution was a gratifyingly justifiable invasion of Normandy; and at Christmas Henry went home to plan it.

Shortly before Easter 1105, Henry returned with a powerful army and landed at Barfleur in the Cotentin. Many of the barons in western Normandy were his loyal supporters, and most of them were tired of anarchy. When Henry attended Mass on Easter Day at Carentan, the Bishop of Sées, who had been driven from his see by Robert of Bellême, pointed to the pathetic possessions which the peasants had brought to the safety of sanctuary and exhorted the king and his barons to save Normandy from its wretchedness. But the conservative bishop was quaintly disappointed by the appearance of his Norman liberators, and he ended his exhortation with such an effective disapproval of their decadent Saxon customs that even the king agreed to have his hair cut.

To meet the invasion the impoverished Duke of Normandy could muster no more than feudal levies, inept commanders like his English friend, Edgar the Atheling, and unscrupulous, defiant vassals like Robert of Bellême and William of Mortain, who were obliged to support him for want of an alternative. Henry had denied him one potential ally by bribing the Count of Flanders to remain neutral, and to strengthen his already superior army he had engaged mercenary cavalry from Brittany and bought the alliance of the counts of Anjou and Maine. Yet, with such an advantage, Henry was initially neither as successful nor as active as he might have been. Although he burned Bayeux and bribed Caen into surrender, he failed to capture Falaise, and in August he went home to England, where he remained for nearly a year while his brother and Robert of Bellême visited him separately to sue in vain for peace and a pardon.

In July 1106, however, Henry returned to the war, and in September he was besieging William of Mortain's town of Tinchebrai, when Duke Robert arrived with his army to relieve it. As he had done at Alton, Henry attempted to negotiate a settlement. He offered to allow Robert to enjoy the income from half the duchy in return for the rest and the right to govern

149

it all; but it was such a humiliating offer that even Robert was proud enough to refuse it. On 28 September 1106, forty years to the day after William the Conqueror had landed in England, an English army commanded by a Norman king fought on Norman soil against a Norman army in which the English pretender to the English throne served as a commander.

Henry and most of his knights fought on foot with the fyrd, while his mercenary cavalry waited in the rear under Count Elias of Maine. Led by William of Mortain, Norman knights charged the English line and nearly broke it, but while they were engaged Count Elias swung round them with King Henry's cavalry and charged into the flank of Duke Robert's infantry. At that crucial moment Robert of Bellême, who commanded the Duke's rearguard, fled from the field, and with his flight the Duke's little army crumbled.

After hardly more than an hour of fighting, the victory at Tinchebrai was total. Normandy and England were again united, and peace was restored to the wretched duchy. All the unlicensed castles were destroyed, all land grants which had been made since the death of William I were cancelled, and the duchy was subjected to the same ruthless fiscal administration as England. After the battle, William of Mortain was blinded and imprisoned for life, Edgar the Atheling was released to live in obscurity until his death in 1125, and surprisingly – and suspiciously, in view of his flight – Robert of Bellême was left at liberty. Duke Robert was sent as a prisoner to Devizes and later to Cardiff, where he died in 1134. In a brutal age it was nevertheless rare for a king to imprison his brother, and although the Pope pleaded on behalf of the man who had once served as a crusader, Henry did not heed him. But the one merciful gesture that Henry did make was almost fatal. Robert had a son and heir called William, who was known as the Clito – the Norman equivalent of the English title Atheling. Instead of imprisoning the boy or worse, Henry left him in Normandy and placed him under the guardianship of Elias of Saint Saens. It was a mistake which he soon learned to regret. To many Normans who accepted Robert's exile, the Clito was his rightful successor, and to all the Normans whom Henry had deprived of their estates, the only hope of regaining them lay in his succession. For the next twenty-two years all Henry's

OPPOSITE Falaise, the birthplace of William the Conqueror, which withstood the first assaults of his son, Henry I, in 1105. The castle was rebuilt by Henry I in 1123, and the round tower was added by the French king, Philip II, Augustus, who conquered Normandy at the beginning of the thirteenth century.

King Louis VI of France, Louis the Fat. A great patron of the church and a courageous soldier, Louis strove unsuccessfully throughout his life to limit the influence of Henry I.

policies in northern France were dominated and determined by the Clito's cause, and obstructed by the rebels and neighbours who supported it.

In July 1108, on the advice of the apprehensive Curia Regis, Henry returned to Normandy to take William the Clito into his own custody. But Elias of Saint Saens refused to hand him over and, after Henry had seized his castle, he travelled through the duchy, hiding the boy and canvassing support until eventually he sought refuge with the new king of France, Louis VI. Louis, who was to be known as Louis the Fat, succeeded his feeble father, Philip I, in 1108 and was crowned a few weeks after Henry's return to Normandy. He was a clumsy diplomat, but he was an energetic and enthusiastic if unremarkable soldier. From the beginning of his reign he was determined to restore his effective suzerainty over the principalities that surrounded his own domains – particularly Normandy and Flanders, which commanded the trade routes between Paris and the Channel.

152

By the time William the Clito reached his court in 1111, Louis was already at war with Henry. In 1109 Henry had garrisoned the border town of Gisors, which he had agreed should remain neutral after his conquest of Normandy; in response, Louis had advanced his army, and only an impassable stretch of the river Epte had prevented a major battle. Since then, French soldiers had been attacking Norman border castles with some success.

In the cause of the Clito, Louis saw his chance to replace Henry with a grateful and less powerful vassal and, as nominal suzerain of Normandy, he declared his support for the Clito's claim. The new count of Anjou, Fulk V, joined him, and so too did the envious Count Robert of Flanders, in spite of the pension which he had been receiving from Henry. When the news reached Normandy, as Louis had hoped, some of the barons, led by Robert of Bellême, William Crispin and the Count of Evreux, fortified their castles in open rebellion.

By his clemency with the Clito and his audacity at Gisors, Henry had surrounded himself with danger. His nephew, Count Theobald IV of Blois and Chartres, whose lands lay between Anjou and the French king's domains, began to attack some of Louis' castles in the west, but his raids were not enough to draw French soldiers away from the Norman border. Henry's military resources were precariously divided between threatened borders and rebellious barons. But by avoiding major engagements he kept his army intact, and by isolating the besieged rebel leaders and bribing their landless allies he slowly suppressed the rebellion. After more than a year most of the rebels, including William Crispin and the Count of Evreux, had been exiled, and Robert of Bellême had at last been sent to perpetual imprisonment in England.

But Henry's success in Normandy was only made possible because the French king and his allies preferred dilatory border raids to a full-scale invasion, and, at the beginning of 1113, he resorted to diplomacy. He arranged to meet Count Fulk of Anjou near the town of Alençon, which he had recently captured from Robert of Bellême. Fulk, who was married to the heiress and daughter of the late Count Elias of Maine, claimed the right to succeed his father-in-law, and Henry – who had bought the support of most of the barons in Maine, and as Duke of Normandy claimed suzerainty over it – offered to recognize Fulk as its count in return for his homage. Fulk's enthusiastic acceptance was won when Henry offered to seal the agreement with a marriage between one of Fulk's daughters and his only legitimate son, William the Atheling, the heir to the throne of England.

It was not the first dynastic marriage which Henry had arranged for his children. He had already married his natural daughter Sibylla to his brother-in-law Alexander I, who had succeeded his brother Edgar as king of the Scots. In 1110 he had betrothed his only legitimate daughter Matilda to no less a husband than the Holy Roman Emperor, Henry V. As King Henry prepared to extend the defence of his dominions from the battlefield to the bedchamber, the king of France was outflanked by potential marriages. In the east, the prestigious alliance with the Holy Roman Empire was dangerous enough, but in the west, with Anjou and Maine added to Blois and Chartres, King Henry's influence dominated King Louis' flank from the Channel to the river Loire. Within weeks of the agreement with Fulk, Louis made peace with Henry at Gisors and acknowledged him as Duke of Normandy and suzerain of Brittany and Maine. These French suzerainties were no more than the Norman dukes had exercised or claimed since the days of the Conqueror, but in the treaty of Gisors they were officially recognized by the King of France. In extricating himself from troubles which he himself had created in the first place, Henry had turned a potential military disaster into a diplomatic triumph.

After suppressing a last pocket of resistance in Bellême, Henry pardoned a few exiles and returned to England. In 1114 he sent his daughter Matilda to Germany to marry the Emperor. But two years later he risked everything by starting the troubles all over again. When his nephew Count Theobald renewed his attacks on the King of France, Henry supported him and sent soldiers, who ravaged the French countryside and captured the castle at Saint Clair.

Henry was devoted to his sister Adela and to three of the sons whom she had borne in her marriage to the late Count of Blois and Chartres. Theobald was her second son, but he had succeeded his father after the eldest, William, who had once sworn an oath in Chartres cathedral that he would kill the

Henry of Blois, who was appointed bishop of Winchester by his uncle, Henry I, in 1126.

bishop, had been discreetly passed over. Her third son, Stephen, had become a constant and favourite member of Henry's court and had been endowed with the county of Mortain after the imprisonment of its former lord; and her fourth son, Henry, was a monk at Cluny. Later in his reign, King Henry was to invest Henry of Blois with an abbey and his richest see, and to endow Stephen of Blois with so many estates that he became almost as rich and influential as Harold Godwinson had been in the reign of Edward the Confessor. In 1116, however, his support for Theobald was excessively reckless.

Again King Louis declared war in favour of William the Clito. The new Count of Flanders, Baldwin VII, joined him; Count Fulk of Anjou, ostensibly angered by the aggression on the border of Blois, abandoned his allegiance to Henry and renewed his alliance with Louis; and this time the barons of Normandy rose in formidable numbers. For two years the armies of Flanders, France and Anjou raided, pillaged and burned along the entire eastern and southern borders of Normandy, and within the borders – under a duke and king

155

archieps dabitis: eps ligna
bruno. eodem die ipso mo
terio uibente papa tria itr
pmus cancellis sacrariut
ria. Tunc papa itr sacndo
sasq; agendo. p alia salutis
tautta. cord epis g cardinalit
multorq; psonus. huicem
habuit ad pptin

The consecration of the third abbey church at Cluny by Pope Urban II in 1095. It was at this great Benedictine monastery that Henry of Blois, the brother of King Stephen, was received into holy orders.

regi uel principi curam ipsius
tutelamq; commendauit. nisi
deo et beato Petro eiusq; uica
rius. romanis scilicet pontificib'
Auox numero uel ordini diuina
me dignatio licet indignum af
sociauit. me olim monachum
prioremq; monasterii huius. sub
domno ac uenerabili hugone

hugo

who had once reproached his brother for the incompetence of his government – the duchy was reduced to as much anarchy as it had suffered under Robert. Barons who had been enemies in private wars divided equally between the Duke and the Clito, and then changed sides as their own interests altered. It was a treacherous, vicious civil war. In the brutality of his conduct the king was no better than the worst of his barons. Eustace of Breteuil, who supported the Clito, was married to one of Henry's natural daughters; as a surety for his suspension of hostilities, Henry forced him to hand over his two young daughters, and in return sent him the son of one of his commanders. When Eustace blinded the boy, Henry retaliated by delivering his own grandchildren to the boy's grieving father, who, with Henry's consent, sent the little girls home to their parents with their eyes put out and their noses cut off.

Henry's second war with his barons and the French allies was a repetition of the first on a much larger scale; but in 1118 Louis lost the ally on his right flank when the Flemish army withdrew after Count Baldwin had been mortally wounded, and in the following year he lost the ally on his left flank when Henry renewed his offer of a marriage to Count Fulk of Anjou. William the Atheling was brought over from England and in June he was married to Fulk's eldest daughter, Isabella, at Lisieux.

With no one left to fight but the rebel barons and the king of France, Henry took the offensive. After burning the rebel town of Evreux, he was advancing towards Louis' headquarters at Les Andelys with 500 of his finest knights, including William the Atheling and his bastards Richard and Robert, Earl of Gloucester, when scouts reported that King Louis and William the Clito were riding out with an equally splendid company of 400. On 20 August 1119, on the plain at Brémule (or Brenneville), the two companies met. It was a small battle, but it was also a glorious chivalric engagement, and it was in magnificent contrast to the atrocious civil war that had been devastating Normandy. Henry dismounted 400 of his knights and drew them up in a line with 100 horsemen on their flank commanded by his son Richard. Before Louis had drawn up his own line, the Norman rebel William Crispin charged forward with eighty knights and drove them so deep into Henry's line that he was able to strike the king, smashing his helmet and drawing blood from his head; but they were surrounded and outnumbered by Richard's knights, and all eighty surrendered. When a second French charge failed, Louis fell back and, as Henry's knights remounted and gave chase, the withdrawal turned into a rout. By the end of the day 140 French knights had been captured and many more, including their king and the Clito, had been unhorsed. But since the knights on both sides were more interested in taking prisoners than causing casualties, only three had been killed. Henry restored most of his prisoners without ransom – even those who were his own vassals – and returned Louis' captured banner and charger, and with the same courtesy William the Atheling sent back the charger of William the Clito.

Humiliated by his defeat, Louis made one last raid into Normandy and then tried to match Henry at diplomacy instead. At the Council of Rheims he pleaded the cause of the Clito before Pope Calixtus II. When the Norman archbishop of Rouen rose to reply, the council refused to listen. But the Pope, who was attempting to make peace with the emperor, was anxious not to offend the emperor's father-in-law; he met Henry at Gisors and, accepting his case, negotiated a peace with Louis. Henry had won another diplomatic triumph: to the alliance with Anjou and the empire, he had added the support of the papacy. The new Count of Flanders, Charles the Good, made peace with him; rebels were pardoned and conquests were restored; and, in place of William the Clito, the king of France accepted the homage of William the Atheling as heir to Normandy.

On 25 November 1120 Henry sailed home to England from Barfleur with his new daughter-in-law. Before he embarked, a captain approached him, claiming that his father had carried Henry's father in 1066 and begging the privilege of carrying Henry in his splendid new vessel, the *White Ship*. Since his own ship was already chosen, Henry granted instead that the *White Ship* should carry his heir and his treasure. When Henry sailed, William the Atheling and his young company were still feasting, and, so that the crew of the *White Ship* might join in their revels, casks of wine were sent on board. By the time she put to sea that evening even her pilot was drunk. Beyond

Text in the manuscript margins:

tag: 141
regnie an
que. Ad
quam ere
peruit
sui annis
tion exiit
deanime.
Neal enim
uouit in
oriencales
partes an
glie sub
uestitum
sci lib
mundis
oris erat
ryni ta
mociun a
implota
duxum.
sinemq;
iustitiam
gastutin
seruens
n.

Barfleur the *White Ship* struck a rock, ripped open her hull,
filled with water and heeled over. Hurriedly the captain placed
William the Atheling in the only boat, but the boat was
submerged by the weight of the panicking crowd that leapt
from the listing hull as the *White Ship* sank. The only survivor
was the poorest passenger, a butcher from Rouen.

Apart from William the Atheling, Henry's bastard Richard
and one of his natural daughters were drowned, and there was
hardly a family at his court which had not lost a young lord or
lady in their company. A day passed before the courtiers dared
to tell the king, and when they did they chose a child as their
messenger. As the son of Count Theobald broke the news, King
Henry fell senseless to the floor.

It was a catastrophe. Queen Matilda had died in 1118; Henry
was a widower without a legitimate son. Unlike his
grandfather, he was too concerned with the legitimacy of his
own title to consider nominating one of his bastards, and it was
impossible to imagine that his subjects or the rest of Europe

tui successit Henricus frater
eius z regnauit annis xxxvi.
Hic erat pastor ferax z custos
memor fuit z sapiens z stre
nuus Dux Normannie que
peruersius ambrosius Leonem iusticie
in historia Regum noiauit ffecit qz eni
iusticium z iusticiam in terra. Dixit qz
Vxorem generosam z optimam de
nobili genere anglorz. z Ordonũ p
quam multum sibi confederauit Reg
num scilicet ffilam pncipis siu Alba
nie Vita z morib3 ornatam sororem
sciliceit Alexandri principis siu Ordoie
z Dauitis Ordoie qui postea fuit princeps
Albanie. Cui vero Rex Henricus pfa
tus dedit honorem de Huntingdon
cum matilda cognate sua que erat
Vxor prius pmi simonis de scensliz
comitis de Huntingdon z Norhing
ton cum custodia puerorz suorz et die
concordes ad inuicem deinde effecti
fuerunt qua predtus Alexander ven
dicauit sibi iure hereditario coronã
z monarchiam totius Regni presti
citer uerus heres z iustus de iure boni
Regis Edwardi ultimi. Dixert qz deu
sup omnia dilauit qz ordam ecclesiam in
multas p locã fecit qz bonũ in eintu
totius malum qz deleuit vocabetur
matilds Regina optima Obiit uo
predictus henricus in Normanniã
apud L. Ionis. sepultus enim fuit
in Anglia apud Redinges in Alba
thia quam construxerat. matilda
vero Regina predicta sepulta fuit
in Anglia apud Westmonasteriũ
cuius anime pricietur deus.

Henricus primus genuit

Willm
qui periit
in mari

Ricm
qui piit
in mari

Matil
dam Im
patrice

Ricard
q obiit

Henria
Regis se
cundi

would allow his kingdom and duchy to devolve through his daughter to the Holy Roman Emperor. William the Clito was now the rightful heir not only to Normandy but to England as well. The resources of a kingdom, careful diplomacy and years of brutal war had all been wasted, and a king's dream of a dynasty that might rule an Anglo-French empire had perished with a prince in a beautiful ship.

The Curia Regis advised Henry to take a second wife at once, and on 25 January 1121 he married Adela, the daughter of Godfrey, Count of Louvain and Duke of Lower Lorraine. But the Norman rebels whom Henry had pardoned began to prepare another rebellion to promote the claims of the Clito, and King Louis and the Count of Evreux suggested to Count Fulk of Anjou that he might still be the grandfather of a duke or even a king if he married the Clito to his second daughter, Sibylla. Fulk was easily persuaded; he was already furious because Henry had returned his widowed eldest daughter without her dowry and had even refused to part with it when Fulk went over to England to collect it himself. In 1123 the marriage between the Clito and Sibylla was consecrated, the Norman rebels rose and Henry was again in Normandy at the head of an army.

This time, however, Henry had powerful allies and the rebels were isolated. Count Charles the Good came to support Henry with the army of Flanders; the Pope annulled the Clito's marriage; and, to keep King Louis from interfering, the Holy Roman Emperor distracted him by massing the German army beyond his eastern borders. The rebels were suppressed with merciless brutality. Many were imprisoned and at least two were blinded first. When Henry also sentenced the poet Luke de Barre to blinding and perpetual imprisonment, his ally, Charles the Good, protested that Luke was not his vassal and had only been fighting for his lord; but Henry had been infuriated by the poet's satires of him, and Luke only saved himself from his fate by bashing his own brains out against the walls of his cell.

Henry's second queen accompanied him during the suppression of the rebellion, but she failed to conceive, and by 1125 it had become obvious that the marriage was going to be childless. Since the death of William the Atheling, it had seemed likely that if Henry died without a legitimate son he would

OPPOSITE A twelfth-century genealogical tree, with illuminations of Henry I and the death of his son, William the Atheling, in the wreck of the *White Ship*.

163

nominate his favourite nephew Stephen of Blois as his heir. With each rebellion, in spite of his policy to the contrary, Henry had endowed Stephen with so many confiscated estates that he was now the richest landlord in Normandy and one of the two richest in England. In 1125 Henry married Stephen to the only daughter and heiress of Count Eustace III of Boulogne, another Matilda, whose mother had been a sister of Henry's first queen and whose father had decided to retire to a monastery. With this marriage Stephen was allied to the royal house of Scotland and acquired not only the county of Boulogne but Eustace's considerable estates around Colchester and London as well.

In the same year, however, the Holy Roman Emperor died. Henry's widowed daughter returned to live with him, and when they went home to England in 1126 he cowed his Curia Regis into accepting her as heiress to his throne. On Christmas Day the king's councillors swore their allegiance to the Empress Matilda. Henry's guest, David, King of Scots, who had succeeded his brother Alexander in 1124, paid homage for his English estates, and the first Anglo-Norman baron to follow him was Stephen of Blois, Count of Mortain and Boulogne, and feudal lord of half a million English acres from Lincolnshire to Kent.

Neither England nor Normandy had ever been ruled by a woman, and the general anxiety which followed the English homage to Matilda induced King Louis to renew his support for William the Clito. As soon afterwards as January 1127 he married the Clito to his queen's half-sister and, in March, when Charles the Good was murdered, he granted the Clito the county of Flanders, on the grounds that he was the eldest grandson of Baldwin v. Henry returned to Normandy, marched an army into France to prevent Louis from supporting the Clito against the rebels who rose to oppose him in Flanders, and renewed his alliance with Anjou by offering Matilda's hand to Count Fulk's son and heir, Geoffrey Plantagenet.

Since the husband of the heiress to a throne could expect to become a king, Fulk and his Angevins were delighted, but for the same reason the marriage was dangerously unpopular elsewhere. On both sides of the Channel the Normans resented the prospect of being ruled by their old enemy from Anjou; the English, who were now resigned to the rule of one foreign

OPPOSITE Geoffrey Plantagenet, Count of Anjou, the second husband of the Empress Matilda and the father of King Henry II, from his tomb in Le Mans cathedral.

dynasty, dreaded the prospect of a new one; Bishop Roger of Salisbury declared that he would never have paid homage to Matilda if he had known she was going to marry a foreigner; and Matilda herself, who had grown haughtily accustomed to being an empress, objected to a husband who was not only the humble heir to a county but also ten years her junior. Nevertheless, Henry ignored the protests: as a woman, Matilda was already an unwelcome successor, and if he was to produce a more acceptable male heir in his own line, her marriage was his only chance.

The marriage, which was delayed until Geoffrey was sixteen years old, was celebrated in 1128. Shortly afterwards William the Clito died from a wound which he had received while fighting against his rebellious new subjects in Flanders. But his death did not secure the succession for Matilda, it only removed the most likely contender; and the provocative marriage showed no sign of producing a more welcome heir. When Henry returned to England he learned that Matilda had quarrelled with her husband and gone to Rouen. During the next two years, while she lived in Normandy and England, the king's councillors were to augment their opposition to her sex and her marriage with a personal distaste for her arrogance. In 1131, however, having succeeded his father, Geoffrey wrote to Henry asking for the return of his wife, and, after forcing his barons to renew their homage to her, Henry gladly sent her back to Anjou. In 1133 the long-awaited news arrived: Matilda had given birth to a son, Henry Plantagenet.

While King Henry was crossing the Channel to meet the boy, the sun was eclipsed, and like the appearance of Halley's comet sixty-nine years before, it was seen as an omen of disaster. When he reached Normandy, Matilda brought her son to live with him at Rouen where, in 1134, she gave birth to her second son, Geoffrey. But the king was not to end his days doting on his grandson in peace. In 1135 his son-in-law demanded several Norman castles which he claimed had been promised to him on his marriage. When Henry indignantly refused, Geoffrey attacked and destroyed the castle of the Viscount of Beaumont, a few Norman renegades rose to support him, and Matilda, objecting to Henry's ruthless retaliation against the rebels, left her father to join her husband. The cruel old king had been scheming and fighting for forty-eight years, and in the sixty-eighth and last year of his life he was at war with his own heirs.

For some time Henry's health had been failing. He was exhausted, and the final petty quarrel with Geoffrey and Matilda made him nervous and depressed. While hunting in the forest of Lyons he was seized by a fever that was said to have been caused by eating lampreys, which his physician had specifically forbidden. When he died in his hunting lodge on the evening of 1 December, the only one of his children beside him was his bastard Robert, Earl of Gloucester. His body was taken home to England and on 4 January 1136 it was buried in the church of the monastery which he had founded at Reading.

Henry had ruled England for thirty-five years. It had been long enough to establish his new judicial and fiscal administration, but not long enough to achieve the continental ambitions into which he had drained the resources of his kingdom. In a few more years he might have accustomed his subjects to accepting his grandson in place of his daughter, and his dream of an empire that included England, Normandy, Brittany, Maine and Anjou would have been fulfilled in the peaceful succession of Henry Plantagenet. But through age and a surfeit of lampreys, the chance was denied him.

Stephanus in Regem magnatum laude Le
proles p legem metaldis post dominat

168

Post morte Regis henrici regula legi
Substituit tota placuit p pre remot

7
'Nineteen Long Winters'

WHEN KING HENRY I died, Normandy dissolved into its accustomed anarchy and Count Geoffrey of Anjou, the alien husband of his chosen heir, advanced an army towards its border. But the defences of the duchy were stronger than usual: the one bond that united the Norman barons was their hatred for their traditional enemy, and most of the equally hostile English barons, who had accompanied the king to Normandy, were standing by to support them with their feudal levies. There was hardly a man among them who was ready to honour the allegiance that he had sworn to the arrogant Empress Matilda; and while their soldiers made ready for battle on the border, the Anglo-Norman barons, like the Witan of the kingdom that their fathers had conquered, assembled to debate the disputed succession. Although their own interest had led them to divide themselves between brothers at the beginning of the two previous reigns, this time, to preserve their independence, they were prepared to combine and compromise.

Apart from King Henry's daughter Matilda, there were four other possible candidates for his throne: his favourite and most powerful bastard, Earl Robert of Gloucester; his grandson, Henry Plantagenet; and two of his nephews, Count Theobald of Blois and Chartres, and Count Stephen of Mortain and Boulogne. Early in the debate the choice was narrowed when Earl Robert, gallantly acknowledging that his own inheritance was barred by his bastardy, declined to stand as a candidate; and although he subsequently declared his support for King Henry's direct, legitimate male heir, Henry Plantagenet, the other barons rejected the child on the grounds that his succession would have meant that his parents, Geoffrey and Matilda, ruled as regents. But the barons who would have opposed Robert also opposed Stephen, since the two were such jealous rivals that the succession of either might have led to the rebellion of the other. Once the choice was limited to the brothers of the house of Blois, the attractions of the least likely candidate became apparent. As the elder, Theobald had the better claim; as an independent count, he could add the rich resources of his counties to the Anglo-Norman armies; and since he did not have Stephen's feudal strength within the kingdom or the duchy, he was more likely to be tractable. In the end, to the surprise of many, the barons of England and Normandy agreed

PREVIOUS PAGES AND OPPOSITE King Stephen, from early fourteenth-century manuscripts.

170

Matilda and her first husband, the Holy Roman Emperor, Henry V, at their wedding feast.

ᔥ ᔥo dm̄ ō. ē. xiiii. lmpr̄ henriē natalē
dm̄ . baben̄b. celebrauīo. dispositis nuptiis suis

to offer their throne to Count Theobald.

What the barons had overlooked, however, was that their opinion was not necessarily decisive. Both William Rufus and Henry I had ascended the throne with the support of only a small circle of baronial friends; it had been the recognition of the Church that had made them anointed kings. In the early years of their reigns, when they defended their thrones against the barons who sought to replace them with their brother, they had relied predominantly on the fyrd rather than on other barons, and it had been the support of the Church, with its social influence, its political power and its feudal levies, that had tipped the balance in their favour. In 1135 the pattern was to be repeated. In the absence of most of the lay tenants-in-chief, England was being governed by the clerical members of the Curia Regis; while those lay tenants-in-chief were preparing to offer the throne to one candidate, and the husband of another threatened them, the successful candidate was in England negotiating with the clergy.

As soon as he heard that King Henry was dead, Stephen sailed from Boulogne to England. Although he was refused entry at

172

Dover and Canterbury, which were garrisoned by the soldiers of Earl Robert, he was welcomed and acknowledged by the citizens of London. From there he sped to Winchester, where his brother, Henry of Blois, had been invested with the bishopric by King Henry in 1126. Bishop Henry was Stephen's vital ally; he secured the support of the treasurer, and with Stephen's promise that he would maintain the freedom of the Church, together with his own guarantee that the promise would be kept, he won over the justiciar, Bishop Roger of Salisbury. When they approached the Archbishop of Canterbury, William of Corbeil, the Archbishop protested that they had all sworn allegiance to Matilda, but he was soon persuaded by the advantages of Stephen's promise, by the argument that the oaths were invalid because they had been made under compulsion, and by the perjury of one of the few barons who were present, Hugh Bigod, who swore that King Henry had changed his mind in favour of Stephen on his deathbed, although he had not been there. On 22 December, in the presence of only two other bishops and a small insignificant gathering of barons, William of Corbeil crowned Stephen in Westminster Abbey.

The Anglo-Norman barons were negotiating the final terms of their allegiance to Count Theobald when a monk arrived with the news that Stephen was already the anointed king. At once they withdrew their offer; the English barons hurried home, and Theobald, disappointedly acknowledging his brother, set out for the army of Anjou, where he negotiated a six months' truce with the Count in Stephen's name. When Matilda appealed to Rome, Stephen's envoys argued contemptibly that she was a bastard because her mother had been a nun, and she was opposed by Count Theobald and also by King Louis, who was eager to prevent the unification of Anjou and Normandy. Although it was to be three years before Pope Innocent II finally rejected her plea, he wrote in the meantime to Stephen, tacitly accepting him as master of England.

In the anxious atmosphere that followed the death of King Henry I, Stephen began his reign with three advantages: in the first place, to most of his barons he was at least an acceptable alternative to Matilda, and as such they were prepared to give him a chance; secondly, unlike his two predecessors, he was

LEFT Rochester castle. The tower-keep, where Earl Robert of Gloucester was imprisoned in 1141, was built by the archbishop of Canterbury, William of Corbeil, soon after 1126.

The elegant west front of the church of Saint Mary the Virgin at Iffley in Oxford.

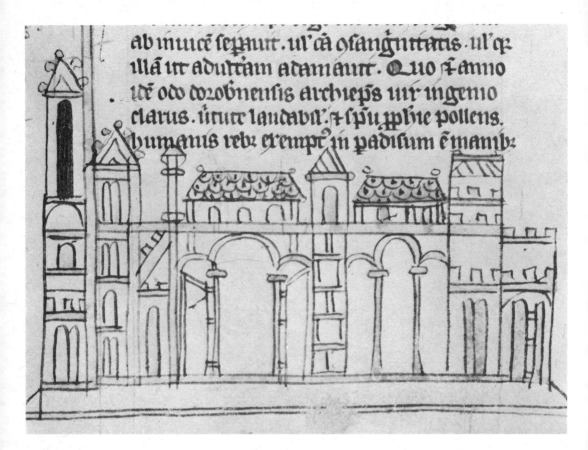

ab in unce sepwitt . ul'ca osanguittatis . ul'ce
illa ur adurram acam auir . Q̃uo ff anno
tr̃ oco cozobnenfis archieps ur ingenio
clarus . fitute laudabil'. + spu̶ ppl̶ie pollens .
humanis reb; ex̃empt̃ in padifum ẽ mamb;

A thirteenth-century
drawing of Westminster
Abbey.

already a rich and powerful feudal lord; and thirdly, unlike any
other Norman king, he was an attractive man and personally
popular. 'When he was a count,' wrote William of Malmesbury, 'by his good nature, and by the way that he sat and ate in
the company of even the humblest, he had earned an affection
that can hardly be imagined.' He was the first king to permit
jousting in England, and his romantic reputation for exemplary
chivalry still survives, although it is not entirely justified. He
could be treacherous, he was capable of cruel blackmail and his
most generous chivalric gestures were performed against his
own inclinations on the advice of others. Nevertheless, he was
gallant by the standards of his time, he was charming, dashing
and courageous, and in the thick of battle he was a formidable
warrior. He had all the qualities of a courtier and a soldier, and
he had both the ambition and the initiative to seize a throne. But
he had none of the qualities of a king or a commander, and he
had neither the ruthlessness nor the determination to retain that

176

precarious throne in peace. When his ruinous reign was over his character and the causes of his failure were well summarized by Gervase of Canterbury, who wrote, 'It was the king's custom to start many endeavours with vigour, but to bring few to a praiseworthy end.'

After their return home, the barons of England watched and waited. Matilda's only certain allies were her husband Geoffrey, Count of Anjou, and her uncle David, King of Scots; but, for logistic and traditional reasons, Geoffrey was more interested in the conquest of Normandy than the conquest of England, and David's support for his niece's cause was more motivated by the opportunities that it provided than by any sense of obligation or justice. David was married to the daughter of the late Earl Waltheof, through whom he had inherited the earldom of Huntingdon, and it was in his capacity as an English earl that he had paid homage to Matilda in 1126. Although another of his nieces was married to Stephen, David's oath to Matilda was an honourable excuse for a campaign to recover the lands that had been lost to William II, to impose his suzerainty on the vacant earldom of Northumbria, which he claimed through his wife, and to conquer anything else that was going while he was about it.

As soon as he heard that Stephen had been crowned, King David invaded northern England. Although Stephen was not yet able to rely on his barons, control of the treasury gave him the money to pay Flemish mercenaries and the English fyrd. With characteristic alacrity, he marched north at the head of an army that was large enough to bring David to negotiate. Then, with equally characteristic lack of resolve, he bought David's worthless support with exorbitant concessions. He ceded Doncaster and Carlisle, with which went most of Cumberland and Westmoreland; he acknowledged David's son Henry as Earl of Huntingdon; and he promised that if he ever revived the earldom of Northumbria Henry should have it. But the speed and apparent success of his actions against the Scots convinced his subjects that he was a determined and capable king. At his prolonged Easter court in 1136, most of the barons and bishops in England swore their allegiance, and by the end of April even Earl Robert of Gloucester had cautiously paid homage on condition that he was allowed to retain his estates.

David I, King of Scots, with his grandson and successor, Malcolm IV.

When the Easter court was over, however, Stephen was faced with his first rebellions. On hearing a rumour that the king was dead, one of his first supporters, Hugh Bigod, seized the castle at Norwich. In Devon, Robert of Bampton, emulating the conduct of his peers in Normandy, began to plunder the vassals of his neighbours. Hugh Bigod surrendered Norwich as soon as Stephen appeared at its gates, and Robert of Bampton's castle was taken easily; but immediately afterwards a more dangerous rebel, Baldwin de Redvers, seized the town and castle of Exeter. Although Baldwin's sympathy lay with the Empress Matilda, whose father had invested his family with most of their English estates, the only evidence of that sympathy had been his absence from the Easter court. On hearing that Earl Robert had paid homage he had gone to the King to follow the example, and it had been Stephen's decision that he should forfeit his estates as a punishment for the tardiness that had driven him to defiance. After a siege of three summer months, Baldwin surrendered Exeter castle when the well ran dry, and, at the request of Earl Robert and the other barons in the besieging army, Stephen reluctantly granted him a pardon. But Baldwin retired to his castle on the Isle of Wight and embarked on a brief career of piracy until, when Stephen and his army appeared on the coast, he surrendered again. This time Stephen allowed him no more than a safe conduct to leave the kingdom and seek refuge in Anjou. So far Stephen had been far more fortunate than his predecessors – the rebellions ended with Baldwin's departure, they had been nothing compared to those at the beginning of the previous two reigns, and not one of them had been prompted by open loyalty to the cause of a contender for his throne.

A penny, minted during the civil war and bearing the head of Henry I's illegitimate son, Earl Robert of Gloucester, the most powerful and competent of Matilda's English supporters.

Towards the end of March 1137, leaving his kingdom at peace, Stephen sailed with Earl Robert to his duchy, where he achieved the semblance of success without any of the substance. He placated his brother Theobald with a pension, he made an alliance with King Louis of France, who readily acknowledged him as Duke of Normandy, and he negotiated a new two-year truce with Count Geoffrey, who invaded his duchy five weeks after he landed. However, it was easier for Stephen to negotiate a truce with Geoffrey than it would have been to defeat him: by the time the truce was proposed Stephen had lost the support of the Norman barons. They had welcomed him enthusiastically when he landed and they had rallied round him eagerly when Geoffrey invaded, but their knights resented his Flemish mercenaries, whom he trusted more than anyone, and as they were advancing to attack Geoffrey, relations between the two forces deteriorated until, after a riot and considerable bloodshed, the barons defiantly withdrew their knights from the king's standard without his permission. Once the truce had been concluded, Stephen and his barons were formally, but not cordially, reconciled through the mediation of the Archbishop of Rouen, and in November, carelessly delegating the suppression of anarchy to Earl Robert and others, Stephen returned to England.

The brief visit to Normandy revealed the king in his true colours. As he should have learned from the example of his uncle, King Henry, the key to retaining control of his kingdom lay in the ruthless suppression of potential enemies and the rigid imposition of his authority on Normandy. But Stephen had done neither. Although Earl Robert had supported him at the siege of Exeter, he had pressed for Baldwin's pardon and he had not been required to fight against Anjou; so far there had been no positive evidence that his allegiance was honest. Yet Stephen left his rival in Normandy, where he could no longer watch him, and where he was exposed to the influence of the Empress. Abandoning Normandy to the anarchy in which he had found it, Stephen allowed it to languish until the inevitable return of Count Geoffrey, and he made no real effort to recover the genuine and vital goodwill of its barons. As their faith in their king diminished, so too did their hatred of the Count of Anjou. By the time Stephen returned from his duchy to his kingdom, the barons of Normandy knew that they could not rely on the king to defend them; Count Geoffrey, like King David, had discovered that he had nothing to lose by his aggression; and the barons of England were beginning to suspect that the king's initial energy was not supported by stamina. 'When the traitors perceived that the king was a mild man and soft and good and did no justice,' wrote the Anglo-Saxon Chronicler, 'then did they all wonder. They had done homage to him and sworn oaths, but they held no faith.'

In the spring of 1138 the letter which a shrewder king might have expected arrived from Normandy: Earl Robert of Gloucester renounced his allegiance to King Stephen. When it became known that the most powerful tenant-in-chief had transferred his loyalty to his half-sister, his friends and his vassals rose to support him. Across the kingdom the castles of Dover, Canterbury, Bristol, Exeter, Dorchester, Ludlow, Shrewsbury and many more closed their gates in defiance and declared for the Empress Matilda.

The centre of the rebellion was Earl Robert's castle in Bristol, but, after inspecting its defences, Stephen decided that it was too strong to take. Instead, ignoring the advice of his most loyal commanders, he wasted his time attacking smaller and more vulnerable castles, from which, as often as not, the rebels escaped to join their allies in Bristol. The only sensible strategic action was taken not by Stephen but by his queen, Matilda of

A coin minted during King Stephen's imprisonment in 1141, bearing the images of the king and his queen.

Boulogne, who brought over her fleet, blockaded Dover and denied Earl Robert the one rebel port in which he might have been able to land. It was a move that probably saved Stephen: in the summer, King David again invaded the north, and if Robert had landed an army at the same time and co-ordinated the resistance of his castles, Stephen's totally committed forces would hardly have been able to hold them both.

Encouraged by the success of a few earlier raids and by the defection of several Norman barons, King David invaded Yorkshire with an army so large that the terrified northern barons assembled at York and began to discuss what terms they might offer to save themselves. But the sick old Archbishop Thurstan shamed them with his courage; he promised that he would order every parish priest to join their army with his congregation, he declared that he would accompany the army himself, even though he was so weak that he would have to be carried in a litter, and he proclaimed a holy war against the

barbarian invaders. By the time the only company of knights that Stephen could spare had arrived, the northern barons had been inspired to fight.

Among those who were saved from ignominy by Thurstan's example and exhortation, there were members of many noble Norman families like Percy and Mowbray, which had become and were now to remain for centuries among the greatest in England. By an ironic coincidence, there were also two whose families were to rise still higher in the kingdom of their enemy: the commander of Stephen's knights was Bernard de Balliol, whose descendant John Balliol was one day to sit on King David's throne, and one of the other barons was Robert de Bruce, whose descendant and namesake was to replace John Balliol, and through whose subsequent descendants of the House of Stuart the thrones of England and Scotland were at last to be united.

Investing the campaign with the aura of a crusade,

LEFT, ABOVE The keep of Dover castle, built between 1180–1190.

Dover castle, one of the first castles built by the Conqueror after his victory at Hastings.

Archbishop Thurstan created a magnificent standard, which was made from a ship's mast mounted on a wagon, crowned by the host in a silver casket, with the banners of Saint Peter of York, Saint John of Beverley and Saint Wilfred of Ripon flying from it. When the armies of England and Scotland met on the plain beyond Northallerton on the morning of 22 August 1138, it was the standard and not the place that gave its name to the first great battle of Stephen's reign.

With only a few horsemen in their rear, most of the English knights dismounted to form a line interspersed with their archers, and King David was preparing to adopt the same formation when his wild soldiers from Galloway, boasting that they could achieve more bare-breasted than knights in armour, rushed forward to attack. As their chief and their front ranks died fruitlessly in a hail of arrows, they fell back, colliding with King David and the knights behind him; in the ensuing rout it was all that King David could do to effect an orderly retreat.

The victory at the Battle of the Standard seriously weakened Matilda's cause, but in the following year Stephen made up for it. Negotiating peace on terms that might not have been worse if his army had been defeated, he granted the earldom of Northumbria to King David's son Henry in return for no more than a contingent of Scots for his army. Then, in pursuance of his one consistent policy, he lost the support of his most powerful ally.

Since the friends and vassals of Earl Robert were in open rebellion in favour of the Empress, it was prudent to suppose that the men most likely to follow the example were those that her father had 'raised from the dust'. At the instigation of various members of the Beaumont family, Stephen therefore began to erode the influence of King Henry's 'new men' by creating 'new men' of his own, whose loyalty, like the Beaumonts', was bought with offices, earldoms and other honours. In 1138 he imported the unknown Abbot Theobald of Bec, whose lay patron was Waleran de Beaumont, Count of Meulan, and at the end of the year he engineered his election to the see of Canterbury, which had been vacant since the death of William of Corbeil in 1136. But the leader of King Henry's 'new men', Bishop Roger of Salisbury, was still so unassailably powerful that Stephen once remarked that he would part with half his kingdom to retain his support. Bishop Roger was by no means a prelate of the new reforming school: he lived like a prince, he built his own castles, he was married, he had arranged honours for his family and he was so arrogant that he issued writs 'on the king's part and on my own'. Although he no longer held office, as a bishop he was still a member of the Curia Regis, and through his family he still controlled the government of England: his nephew Alexander was Bishop of Lincoln, another nephew, Bishop Nigel of Ely, was the treasurer, and his son, Roger le Poer, was the chancellor.

Again at the instigation of the Beaumonts, who convinced him that Bishop Roger and his family could no longer be trusted, Stephen devised a scheme to ruin them. In June 1139 he summoned them to his court at Oxford, where their personal guards were provoked into an incident in which a man was killed. Calling upon them to answer for the disturbance of his peace, he ordered their arrest, in spite of the fact that they were under the protection of his court, and demanded the surrender of their many castles. The only one to escape was Alexander, who fled to his uncle's strongest castle at Devizes. When Stephen arrived to besiege it he brought his prisoners with him and threatened to hang Roger le Poer unless the garrison surrendered, but the chancellor's father persuaded him to relent by promising to fast until the castle fell. After watching the old bishop starve beneath the walls for three days, his mistress induced his garrison to open the gates. Stephen was so pleased with the success of the blackmail that he tried it again, and when they saw their lord starving, Bishop Alexander's own castles at Newark and Sleaford surrendered also.

Once their temporal power had been destroyed by the capture of all their castles, Bishop Roger and his family were released. The dean of the college of Beaumont-le-Roger was appointed to the office of chancellor, and a new seal was made to distinguish the writs of the new administration. But the clergy were outraged at the persecution of the bishops, and in the king's brother, Bishop Henry of Winchester, they had a powerful advocate. After the death of William of Corbeil, Henry had confidently expected to succeed him; when Theobald was elected in his place he had appealed to Rome, and the Pope had compensated him with the commission of papal

legate, which made him the archbishop's superior. Still smarting at the slight, Bishop Henry summoned a legatine council at Winchester on 29 August and called the king to appear before it to answer to the charge of violating the privilege of the church. When Stephen's chamberlain and advocate pleaded, however, that the bishops had been arrested and punished only in their capacity as the king's ministers, many of the councillors were convinced, including the Archbishop of Rouen, who added that castles could hardly be described as Church property. The council broke up without a clear judgement and with both dissatisfied parties threatening to appeal to Rome.

If not entirely vindicated, Stephen had at least avoided a humiliating condemnation, and with insincere promises that he would make amends, he recovered the ostensible loyalty of his brother. But he could not have chosen a worse time to alienate the sympathy of the rest of the Church and thereby deny himself the support of its feudal levies. Twenty-nine days after the council broke up, the Empress Matilda and Earl Robert of Gloucester landed safely in Sussex.

While Robert set out for the headquarters of the rebellion at Bristol, Matilda installed herself in the castle at Arundel as the guest of the queen dowager and her second husband, and Stephen, who had been attacking other rebels in Dunster and Marlborough, advanced to capture her. But Arundel Castle, which had been built by Robert of Bellême, was strong enough to survive until a rebel army arrived to relieve it, and Bishop Henry persuaded his brother that it would be better to allow his opponents to congregate in one place, so that they could all be defeated at a single blow. Chivalrously, but foolishly, Stephen granted Matilda safe passage to Bristol.

If it was honest, Bishop Henry's advice was at best misguided. The only chance of deciding the issue at a single blow lay in the capture and imprisonment of the Empress. Stephen had already shown that he lacked the determination to invest Bristol, and it was no longer easy to entice an unwilling enemy into open battle. The kingdom was now covered with castles, so long as soldiers survived behind their walls the fighting could be prolonged; and prolonged it was.

Soon after she reached Bristol, every bishop in England save

A gold and gilded silver reliquary of the True Cross, decorated with gems, coloured glass and pearls. According to tradition, it was presented by the Empress Matilda to the abbey of Valasse, which she founded, and where she was to die in 1167.

OPPOSITE Norman arches in the north transept of Winchester cathedral, built between 1079–1093.

187

Richmond castle in Yorkshire, begun before 1089.

Henry of Winchester declared for Matilda, and as more castles were built hurriedly with forced labour and the disinherited barons whose lands had been granted to Stephen's 'new men' rose to oppose him, the rebellions developed into a full-scale civil war. At the courts of King Stephen and the Empress, barons sold their allegiance for lands, titles and offices. A few bargained with both without loyalty to either, and some, without any military purpose, behaved no better than bandits. The authority of the guardians of the king's peace was lost in the turmoil of war. Rape, robbery, kidnapping, murder and hideous torture became as common as petty larceny. Villages were rased, farms were burned, cattle were slaughtered, and unharvested crops were left to rot with the leaves of successive autumns. In the devastation and ensuing famine thousands starved and the homeless built huts in the churchyards, where they lived off roots and the flesh of dogs. 'To crown all these evils', wrote the chronicler of the *Gesta Stephani*, 'England was swamped by a bestial horde of barbarians who had come together simply for the sake of the fighting. In the face of so much suffering they had neither bowels of compassion nor feelings of human pity.' During the next eight years – not

188

everywhere, but in the areas that were ravaged by war or reduced to the same selfish anarchy that had prevailed for so long in Normandy – the people of England were subjected to the bloodiest misery that they have ever endured, and in the words of the *Anglo-Saxon Chronicle*: 'Christ and his saints slept.'

With the loss or gain of a few castles and the gradual growth of Matilda's party, the war dragged on for over a year until, at the end of 1140, Earl Ranulf of Chester and his half-brother, whom Stephen had recently created Earl of Lincoln, deserted him and seized Lincoln's royal castle. While Stephen besieged the Earl of Lincoln in the castle, the Earl of Chester rode to the Earl of Gloucester for help, and on 2 February 1141 Earl Robert and his army appeared beyond the city. Although his own army was much smaller, Stephen marched out to meet him; and although his mounted barons fled, the wings of his army were routed and its centre was surrounded, he fought on, holding his enemies at bay with his sword until the blade broke and then with an axe until the shaft shattered and he fell, stunned by a stone that had been flung from behind him.

Stephen was taken to Bristol where he was imprisoned in chains, and throughout his kingdom his allies abandoned him. King David came south and paid homage to his niece Matilda for his English shires. Bishop Henry admitted her to Winchester and, after summoning a council, declared that the clergy had elected her queen. In Normandy the barons offered the duchy to Count Theobald, who declined and suggested in vain that it should be surrendered to Anjou in return for the release of his brother. In England the only areas that remained loyal to Stephen were his queen's estates in Essex and parts of Kent, where his queen and William of Ypres, the commander of his beloved Flemish mercenaries, held out valiantly and strove to muster a new army.

But the Empress Matilda was never crowned; her wilful arrogance was as much of a handicap as Stephen's irresolution. Ignoring the protestations of Earl Robert, King David and an already disillusioned Bishop Henry, she cancelled most of the grants that had been made by King Stephen, and soon many powerful barons began to repent their recent submission. On entering London she imposed such a heavy tax on the citizens that they rose in arms and marched on her palace in

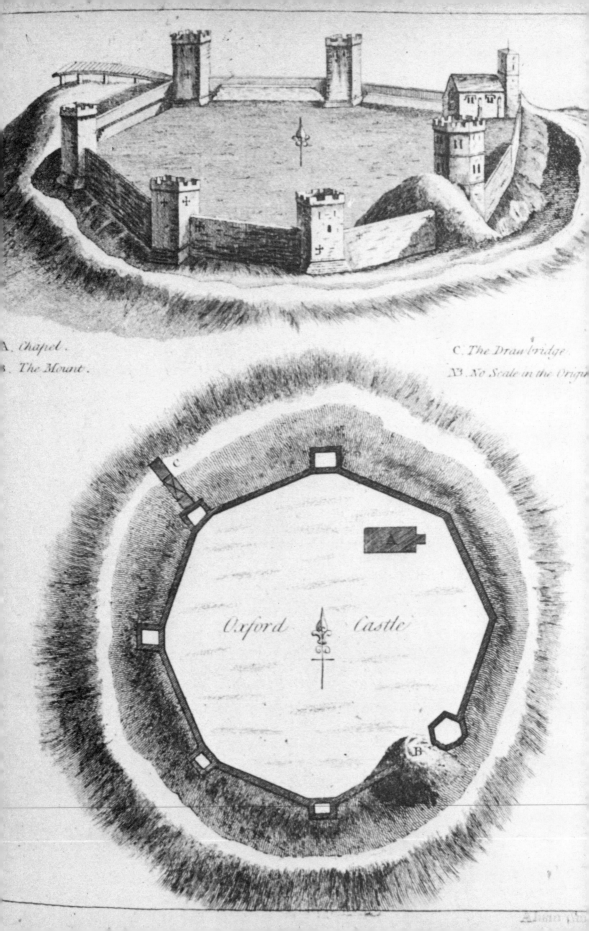

A. Chapel.
B. The Mount.

C. The Drawbridge.
NB. No Scale in the Origi.

Oxford Castle

Saint George's Tower, one of the limestone towers of Oxford castle.

OPPOSITE Oxford castle; a late eighteenth-century engraving.

Westminster. Humiliatingly abandoning the banquet that had been prepared to celebrate her imminent coronation, Matilda and her party summoned horses and set out for her headquarters and her army at Oxford. As she fled, Bishop Henry deserted her, and behind her the queen and the Flemish mercenaries occupied London in the name of the captive Stephen.

While Matilda was in Oxford investing her supporters with earldoms and preparing to recapture London, she discovered that Bishop Henry was negotiating with the queen from Winchester. Accompanied by King David and Earl Robert, she took the town with a surprise attack and laid siege to the Bishop's castle at Wolvesey. But the Bishop escaped and sped for help to London, where the queen had recovered the vital support of Geoffrey de Mandeville, Earl of Essex, who had been one of the most powerful members of Stephen's party before his capture and had returned discouraged from Oxford to renew his allegiance. Led by William of Ypres, the only commander in the king's party who was a match for Earl Robert, the Flemish mercenaries, the queen's soldiers from Boulogne, a contingent of the fyrd from London and the feudal levies of Geoffrey de Mandeville marched on Winchester to besiege the besiegers. On 14 September 1141, as their blockade tightened, Matilda broke through with her vanguard, and King David, who was captured three times and three times bribed his way to freedom, followed her. At the end of the day, however, the gallant Earl Robert, who had initiated their escape and borne the brunt of the fighting in covering it, was a prisoner in the hands of the queen.

The balance that had been lost at Lincoln was restored at Winchester. Without her most competent commander and her most powerful English ally, Matilda was impotent. When Earl Robert honourably resisted all his captors' generous temptations to transfer his allegiance, they arranged to exchange him for the king. On 1 November, Stephen was released from Bristol; two days later, Robert was released from Rochester; and the war continued.

With his magnanimity towards those who had deserted him, Stephen soon restored the strength of his army and even recovered the support of the frightened clergy, who recognized him in a synod at Westminster on 7 December. Matilda's supporters were threatened with excommunication, and in desperation she turned to her husband. But when Earl Robert visited Count Geoffrey in 1142, the Count was engaged in a surprisingly successful invasion of Normandy, and although Robert assisted him in the capture of eleven castles, Geoffrey's soldiers were so fully committed that his only gesture of support was to send the nine-year-old Henry Plantagenet to live for a while with his mother.

In Robert's absence Stephen took the offensive, besieging Matilda in her headquarters at Oxford. Even after Robert returned to distract him by attacking his castle at Wareham, he refused to be drawn away from the siege. But on a December night shortly before Oxford Castle surrendered, when the river was frozen and the fields were covered with snow, Matilda and four knights, dressed in white, climbed down from a tower on a rope and slipped unnoticed through Stephen's lines.

For the next five years the war was a miserable stalemate. In some areas barons on both sides protected their own interests with private treaties, and in others Stephen's soldiers were diverted by renegades like Geoffrey de Mandeville who fought for themselves. Before his brief defection to Matilda, Geoffrey had kidnapped the sister of the new, young King Louis VII of France, Princess Constance, who had been brought to England to marry Stephen's elder son Eustace, and he had held her prisoner for several weeks in the Tower of London. Although the queen had been prepared to overlook the impertinence in order to recover his support, Stephen had remained eager for vengeance, and in 1143 he summoned the unsuspecting earl to his court at Saint Albans and deprived him of all his castles. With his already notorious mercenaries, the furious Geoffrey de Mandeville seized Ramsey Abbey as a base, sacked Cambridge and Saint Ives, and viciously plundered the surrounding countryside until, in the summer of 1144, a stray arrow ended a career that had begun to rival that of Robert of Bellême.

In spite of the diversions, Matilda's outlying castles were slowly reduced, some of her allies were bribed or bullied into desertion and her own enthusiasm began to wane. When Earl Robert of Gloucester died at the end of October 1147, she lost all hope of the English throne, and early in the following year she left the kingdom for ever.

But the civil war did not end with the departure of Matilda. Stephen had already made his fatal mistake in 1137 when he abandoned Normandy. By the summer of 1145, Count Geoffrey had conquered the entire duchy and the recognition of the king of France had been bought with the cession of the Norman Vexin. To the many barons in England who were also tenants-in-chief in Normandy, the price of their continued loyalty to Stephen was the forfeiture of their Norman estates, and since it was impossible to imagine that Stephen would ever reconquer the duchy, their only hope of retaining their estates on both sides of the Channel lay in paying their homage to the house of Anjou and continuing to fight for its success in England. The streams of desertion had not all been flowing in

The White Tower, the keep of the Tower of London. Commissioned by William the Conqueror in 1078, it was built by a Norman monk called Gandulf and took twenty years to complete.

OPPOSITE The chapel of Saint John the Evangelist in the White Tower.

one direction: Matilda's party was still stronger than her spirit. From the moment that her husband's victory seemed certain, many, including most of the Beaumonts, had quitted the king's camp to join her. When she left England, they did not return their allegiance to Stephen; instead they transferred it to a new contender from the House of Anjou – Henry Plantagenet.

Henry Plantagenet's first engagement in the civil war had been a pathetic failure. Having left England in 1146, the fourteen-year-old boy had returned at the beginning of 1147 with a small army of mercenaries which he had neither the funds to finance nor the competence to command. After his attacks on two castles had been repelled he had gone back to Normandy, and according to the hardly credible story in the *Gesta Stephani*, it had been the king who gave him the money to pay for his soldiers and his passage home. When he tried again in 1149 he emulated Stephen, buying the support of King David by confirming all the grants that Stephen had made to him, and since this offended Earl Ranulf of Chester – who had only deserted Stephen in the first place because Carlisle, which his father had been forced to relinquish by Henry I, had been

among those grants – Henry compensated him with the splendid promise of Lancaster instead.

These two northern allies did nothing to dislodge Stephen's hold over the midlands and the south-east of England, where most of Henry's new supporters were powerless behind the walls of their beleagured castles. When they joined Henry to march on York, Stephen came to meet them so quickly and with such a large army that they divided and retreated without offering battle. Nevertheless, Henry was learning fast from his mother's mistakes and his own failures: he knew that the war could not be won with endless sieges, and the experience at York and a subsequent narrow escape had taught him that, until he could match Stephen in open battle, he was only endangering his own freedom by remaining in England. At the beginning of 1150 he withdrew to Normandy to muster an invading army; in spite of the pleas that came from his supporters, he did not return for three years. By then the balance of fortune had shifted.

In Henry's absence Stephen attempted to secure the succession for his son Eustace by having his heir crowned during his own lifetime. But to do this he required the agreement of Archbishop Theobald, and by now he had recklessly renewed his quarrel with the Church. After the death of Thurstan he had appointed his nephew William to the see of York and, in spite of a threat of excommunication, he had refused to depose him in favour of the Church's candidate, Henry Murdac, Abbot of Fountains, who had been consecrated by Pope Eugenius III. Although Stephen relented in 1150 and recognized Henry Murdac in place of his nephew, the implacable pope forbade Eustace's coronation. When all attempts to persuade him failed, Henry summoned his bishops to London in April 1152 and ordered them to crown his son, but they remained obedient to the papal injunction, protesting defiantly that the pope had issued it because Stephen had obtained the throne through perjury. When he tried to frighten them by locking them up, it only served to strengthen their resolve. Emboldened by the support of Rome, the English Church, which had given Stephen his throne, was now ready to take it away from his son.

A month later the queen died, and Stephen lost the steadfast friend who had saved him from the consequences of earlier folly. In grief and bitter disappointment he returned to the war with a new, desperate energy, knowing that only total victory would secure the succession for his son. But the treasury was exhausted and the opposition was stronger than ever; Rome and the English Church were firmly behind the Angevin contender; and, furthermore, the Angevin contender was no longer a landless and penniless figurehead. Henry's father had died in 1151, and in 1152 he had married Eleanor, heiress to the rich duchy of Aquitaine, whose unhappy marriage to King Louis VII had recently been dissolved on the grounds of consanguinity. As Count of Anjou, Duke of Normandy and Duke of Aquitaine, Henry Plantagenet was now the richest and most powerful feudal prince in France.

In January 1153 Duke Henry landed in England with an army of no more than 140 knights and 3,000 infantry. In spite of his new power he had been obliged to leave the bulk of his army to defend Normandy, which King Louis had twice unsuccessfully invaded since his succession: the first time in an attempt to recover the duchy for his brother-in-law Eustace, and the second time in a royal rage because his nominal vassal had married his former wife without his permission. Nevertheless, when Duke Henry reached Devizes, he was joined by the earls of Chester, Hereford, Cornwall and Salisbury, and soon afterwards he was joined by many more, including some of the lesser barons from the midlands who had long been loyal to Stephen.

At last the protagonists were ready to decide the issue in a single battle. But the barons on both sides were afraid that a total victory might be followed by ruinous retribution; when the armies of the King and the Duke met at Malmesbury and again at Wallingford six months later, they persuaded them to hold back. Archbishop Theobald of Canterbury and Bishop Henry of Winchester meanwhile strove in vain to negotiate a settlement until, on 17 August, the sudden and apparently natural death of Eustace removed the one barrier to a compromise. Broken in heart and in spirit, Stephen was no longer interested in the succession, and since his second son William had never expected the throne, Bishop Henry could offer it to Duke Henry with a clear conscience.

On 6 November 1153 the civil war in England was ended by

Pres henry regna Este
uen sun neuou. xix. anz
e morust. e gyst a fauers
ham.

Apres Esteuen regna
le secund henry fi
de sa sozour Lemperice le
quele henry lozs estoyt
dunk de Wozmudy een
son tes fu seyt thomas
Wartyrize. e regna xxxb
ou. xxxb. aunz. puis mo
rust e gyst a sfur E iard.

King Stephen and his successor, Henry II, whom he acknowledged at the
treaty of Winchester in 1153, from a fourteenth-century manuscript.

the Treaty of Winchester. Stephen's private estates were reserved for his son William, and Duke Henry was acknowledged as the heir to his throne. The Duke and his supporters paid homage to the King, and the King's supporters paid homage to the Duke. Mercenaries were dismissed, and together Stephen and Henry began to restore order in the wretched kingdom, disarming allies and enemies alike, returning estates to those that had held them in the reign of Henry I and destroying the unlicensed castles, of which, according to the chroniclers, there were now more than 1,000.

By the beginning of April 1154 the King and the Duke had quarrelled, and, claiming that William and the dismissed Flemish mercenaries were plotting to murder him, Henry returned to Normandy to wait for Stephen's death. He did not have to wait long. For seven months Stephen ruled alone in peace and made a solemn progress through his kingdom, enjoying in defeat the pomp and majesty that he had been unable to win and hold for himself. On 25 October he died, and in the Cluniac abbey which he had founded at Faversham the last Norman king was buried beside his wife and his elder son.

The rule of the proud Norman conquerors had ended in ruin. It seemed as though everything that Henry I had achieved had been destroyed by the charming usurper of his throne. But beneath the chaos the resilient institutions which Henry had fostered had endured, and the carefully sown seeds of his continental empire had survived in Henry Plantagenet. Under the guidance of this grandson they were to flourish and multiply beyond Henry's wildest dreams. The good government of his kingdom was restored, his laws and institutions were revived and expanded into the foundations of a legal system that was to rival Rome's, and through the acquisition of domains and dominions by marriage, diplomacy and force of arms, the Angevin heir to the Norman throne became master of western Europe from the Cheviots to the Pyrenees.

8
The Norman Legacy

WHEN THE NORMANS conquered England, they brought a new Latin culture to a people whose culture was almost purely Teutonic. In Europe, the Teutonic tribes that moved westward into the remnants of the Roman Empire had assimilated some of the Latin culture of the provinces in which they settled. But Britain had been abandoned by the Romans, and in the kingdoms created by the waves of Angles, Saxons, Jutes and Danes who followed, a separate society had evolved. Its traditions were the traditions of a Scandinavian world which the Romans had never ruled, and the only Latin influence came with its conversion to the Roman religion. Under the Anglo-Saxon kings a rich and remarkable Nordic culture flourished and England acquired the distinctive local courts, written laws, regulated currency and elaborate system of taxation which were to survive the subsequent conquest of the Danes. By the middle of the eleventh century the isolated and declining Anglo-Danish kingdom was still a more complex, free and civilized state than simple, centralized and belligerent Normandy.

With their romantic idealization of the Anglo-Saxon era, most of the English historians of the nineteenth century regarded the Norman Conquest as an unmitigated disaster. But, by 1066, Anglo-Saxon art, learning and literature were long past their peak, and the authority of the crown and its institutions had been eroded by the growing power of the earls. Between the departure of the legions and the arrival of the Normans, the Anglo-Saxon civilization had run its natural course through flowering to decay. With the victory of its last successful invaders, the kingdom that had once been the north-west frontier province of the Roman Empire was suddenly restored to a Latin world that was emerging from the Dark Ages with greater vigour and invention. The Normans were not radical innovators; they were shrewd, diligent and conservative developers. In all the lands that they conquered they adopted and adapted the ideas and institutions of their new subjects and introduced others that they had learned from their neighbours or experience. They destroyed little that was worth retaining and only changed where change was necessary; although much of what they added was oppressive and harsh, some of it was enriching or vital. In England their conquest was

PREVIOUS PAGES A fifteenth-century representation of the battle of Hastings. (Ms. Bodley 968, f. 173)

simply the cruel catalyst that fused Anglo-Saxon and Latin traditions to form the foundations of a formidable, united and unique European kingdom. It was only a disaster for the Anglo-Saxon and Danish generations that endured it; the rewards were reserved for their descendants in the centuries that followed.

At the end of Stephen's reign the king's writs were still addressed to 'French and English' subjects, but by then the distinction was less significant than the nineteenth-century romantic would have liked to believe: whether conquerors or conquered, free men were equal in the eyes of the law, and apart from members of the noblest families, there was hardly a Norman who had not married a son or a daughter to a Dane or a Saxon. There was still some resentment on one side and some contempt on the other, but on the whole English society was divided as much by class and culture as it was by race. To the reserved, pretentious, wine-drinking Normans, the new courtly chivalry of Latin Europe was more impressive than the merry informality of the ale-drinking English. They might adopt their laws and their institutions, but they were not prepared to adopt many of their customs.

At court and in the castles, the manners, the conventions, the dress and above all the language were French. While Latin remained the language of the clergy and therefore the bureaucracy, Anglo-Saxon was reduced to little more than the peasant *patois* of the conquered people. But in the conversation of humble men it lost its genders and inflections, and it increased its vocabulary from the language of masters who disdained to speak it. From their Norman commanders the soldiers of the fyrd learned the French terminology of war, and in the kitchens of castles servants who had known animals only as 'sheep' or 'cows' wrapped their tongues round French to call the carcasses 'mutton' or 'beef' when they handed them roasted to the Norman pages. In the end it was the language of the conquerors that faded and the language of the conquered that survived. After more than 300 years, when the Norman kings and their Angevin heirs had gone, the formal, structured Anglo-Saxon of Bede, simplified and enriched, emerged to become the supple, elegant English of Chaucer.

In the countryside, even in those areas that had not been

ETVR:CASTELLVM:AT·HESTENG̃A CEASTRA

Building a castle at Hastings after the Norman landing, from the Bayeux Tapestry.

devastated by reprisals or the civil war, serfs and evicted thegns were oppressed by the exactions of greedy and efficient new landlords. But in the towns, the Saxon and Danish merchants survived, and in time their trade increased. As larger numbers of merchants from France and Italy began to arrive, the export of English wool, tin, hides and corn expanded into new markets, and other commodities were imported from the Mediterranean as well as the Baltic. Enterprising barons promoted fairs in every shire, and guilds of merchants and craftsmen emerged in London and the lesser commercial centres. In the towns of eastern England, like Stamford, Lincoln and Beverley, the immigration of Flemish weavers and the import of dyes led to the manufacture of English cloth, and merchants who had previously been no more than the exporters of raw materials became the first captains of a rich English industry.

To finance their expanding commerce and the construction of castles, cathedrals and abbeys, the merchants, barons and prelates pledged their future incomes for ready cash and, since the northern European Christians still regarded usury as a sin, they borrowed from Jews. Encouraged by William the

OPPOSITE The nave of Durham cathedral, the innovative masterpiece of the Norman architects.

memmit sibilla dicet: turris aū alutuco cui casa diuise st lingue. duo milia cētum septuag
ere dicū passum: paulaū altni angustior coartata erat. ut pondus imminēs et alt sustētaret

Hanc turrē. nembroth gigas construxit. Qui p̄ confusionē ligua
rū migrauit īde ad ipsas. eosq̄ igne colere docuit.

An English ivory carving of the deposition, c. 1150.

Conqueror, Jews from Rouen migrated to London; they were regarded as the personal serfs of the king and by the reign of Stephen they had begun to settle in provincial towns. Their houses became banks, and for security, like those that survive in Lincoln, they were the first houses of ordinary citizens to be built of stone. Like the Flemish weavers, the Jews were envied for their wealth, but their new service was an essential ingredient of the burgeoning, bourgeois capitalism of England, and without it the sudden architectural renaissance would have been impossible.

Borrowing against the incomes of estates that were larger and richer than their estates in Normandy, the barons and prelates also built in stone. At first the castles of England, like the castles of Normandy, were only large mounds, crowned with timber towers and surrounded by ditches and stockades. It was not until the middle of the twelfth century that stone towers began to dominate the thatched roofs of English towns, as the Conqueror's White Tower already dominated London. But

OPPOSITE Saxon craftsmen at work; the building of the Tower of Babel, from a Saxon bible.

207

from the outset the houses of God were built of stone, and it was in the astonishing number of churches, abbeys and cathedrals that rose throughout the kingdom that the Normans manifested their wealth and supremacy. Reflecting the patronage of men whose instincts were the instincts of military engineers, the earliest of these buildings were massive and simple, and the workmanship of the Saxon masons was often dangerously incompetent; but as the skills of the craftsmen improved and the tastes of their masters mellowed, the austerity of the cathedral at Winchester developed into the decorated refinement of the church at Peterborough.

The Normans built with a grandeur that was unrivalled: the nave of Winchester Cathedral was the longest in western Europe, and William II's hall at Westminster was the largest. They were so rich that when towers collapsed they could afford to rebuild them – and they could afford to experiment. At the end of the eleventh century it was the Normans in England and not the French or the Italians who added a new dimension to European architecture. In the cathedral at Durham they built the first high stone roof above a nave to be supported by a groined vault with ribs and pointed transverse arches, and for the first time it became possible to weaken the walls below with windows. The one legacy of the Anglo-Saxon era which the Normans almost obliterated was the achievement of its architects. Some of their rural parish churches survived, but by the end of the Norman rule, almost every abbey and cathedral in England had been rebuilt.

In the twelfth century monks and scholars arrived in the wake of the reforming church and its rich lay patrons. Missionaries of the Norman order of Savigny were followed by the Cistercians, with whom they merged, monasteries were founded or revived in every shire, and, around 1131, an entirely English order for nuns and canons was founded in Lincoln by Gilbert of Sempringham. By the end of Stephen's reign the order of Sempringham had expanded to include another ten houses, and by the time Gilbert died in 1184 it contained 700 canons and 1,500 sisters.

It was Gilbert of Sempringham who also founded the only school for all the boys of a parish. Elsewhere education was expensive and considered unnecessary for ordinary laymen; but

OPPOSITE Westminster Hall. The lower walls are still those that were built by William II. 283 feet long and 68 feet wide, it was the largest in western Europe, but, according to Henry of Huntingdon, the king did not think that it was big enough.

The Church in Norman England

The twelfth century was an age of flourishing monasticism. Under the rule of the Norman kings, every archbishop of Canterbury was a monk. Men and women from all walks of life were drawn to the discipline of the cloisters; and as monks, teachers arrived from Europe to serve the English church which William I and Lanfranc had reformed, the spiritual and intellectual life of the kingdom was revived. By the end of the Norman rule, more than seventy new monasteries had been founded in England and Wales, and English scholars were again studying at the great schools of Europe.

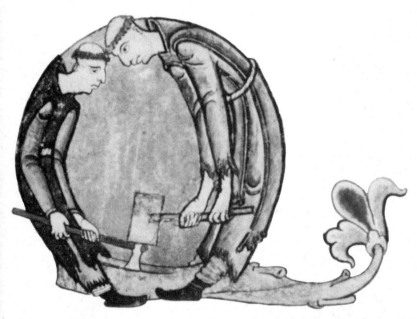

LEFT Monks chopping wood, from a twelfth-century Cistercian manuscript.

BELOW Scholars sitting in a ring around their teachers at Canterbury, from a twelfth-century psalter.

RIGHT A self portrait by the Anglo-Norman illuminator, Hugo Pictor, c. 1100. (Ms. Bodley 717, f. 287v)

RIGHT BELOW The carved ivory head of a pastoral staff, c. 1180.

at a higher level, learning revived. English scholars studied in Latin Europe: many like John of Salisbury studied under no less a man than Peter Abelard, the greatest medieval teacher of theology and the liberal arts, and a clever clerk from Cheapside called Thomas Becket studied law in Bologna. As the scholars returned with other teachers, the intellectual life of Norman England was enhanced by the new curiosity and classical scholarship that came from Norman Sicily, where the old learning of Greece and the new science of Islam had been introduced to parochial and superstitious Christendom. New schools of higher learning emerged in cathedral cities; by the end of the century, the city of Oxford – where the Norman theologian, Theobald of Etampes, began to lecture in 1117 – had become the chief seat of clerical education in England and a centre of intellectual activity. The seeds of a university had been sown.

Archbishop Theobald's attempt to found a school of law was thwarted when King Stephen forbade his Mantuan jurist to lecture. But there was less need for Latin law than other subjects. As they did with the other institutions of government, the Normans adopted and developed the system that they inherited from the Anglo-Saxons; their only innovation was trial by battle. Although they introduced the jury of presentment, which was composed of twelve men who were sworn to bring all the suspected criminals in each hundred before the itinerant justice, the system was no novelty to the Anglo-Saxons, who had once used it themselves.

As Europe emerged from the Dark Ages, the influences of the reforming Church, the monastic revival and Romanesque architecture would have reached England in the end. Without the Normans, the institutions of law, learning and government might well have developed as they developed elsewhere. But without Norman energy and Norman wealth, none of these things would have happened so swiftly or on such a scale. Under the Normans, England began to evolve the governmental institutions of a modern state before any other country in Europe; they gave it a monarchy that was only rivalled in its authority by the Norman monarchy in Sicily; and they bequeathed it an empire that was to take Europe a hundred years of war to destroy. In eighty-eight years they turned a

long-beleaguered island into an unassailable fortress, and long before the conquered had absorbed their conquerors, the invaded had become invaders. Yet the Normans reorganized England's institutions in order to rule it more surely, they reformed its society in order to exploit it and, in the civil war and the pursuit of their continental ambitions, they almost ruined it. Although they were responsible for the change, they can hardly claim credit for the consequences. In the terms of their time, their conquest of England was simply their largest and most surprising territorial expansion; but in the retrospective analysis of history, it was the watershed that marked the emergence of a new power in Europe.

Trial by battle, an 'ordeal' introduced by the Normans, whereby a defendant and his accuser fought before the court, in the belief that God would defend the right. The belief, however, was not unqualified: barons were often represented by one of their vassals, and women and priests were allowed to choose champions.

213

Chronology

1066	(6 January) Harold is crowned King of England.
	(14 October) William the Conqueror defeats Harold at the Battle of Hastings.
	(25 December) William is crowned King of England.
1069–70	William devastates the northern shires.
1070	Lanfranc is created Archbishop of Canterbury.
1075	The rebellion of the earls of Hereford and Norfolk is suppressed.
1078	William's eldest son, Robert, rebels in Normandy.
1086	Special Commissioners carry out the Domesday Survey.
1087	(9 September) William dies. He is succeeded as duke of Normandy by Robert and as king of England by his third son, William Rufus.
1088	William II suppresses a baronial rebellion led by his uncle, Odo, Bishop of Bayeux and Earl of Kent.
1089	Archbishop Lanfranc dies.
1090	William II invades Normandy.
1092	He conquers and settles Carlisle and Cumbria.
1093	Anselm is created Archbishop of Canterbury.
	Malcolm III, King of Scots, is killed near Alnwick.
1095	William II suppresses a second baronial rebellion.
1096	Robert mortgages Normandy to William II and leaves for a crusade.
1100	(2 August) William II is killed in the New Forest.
	(5 August) His younger brother, Henry, is crowned.
1101	Henry and Robert conclude a treaty at Alton.
1106	(28 September) Henry defeats Robert at the Battle of Tinchebrai and becomes master of Normandy.
1107	Henry and Archbishop Anselm settle the investiture dispute.
1109	Archbishop Anselm dies.
1113	Henry concludes a treaty at Gisors with King Louis VI of France, who recognizes him as ruler of Normandy, Brittany and Maine.
1114	Henry's daughter, Matilda, marries the Holy Roman Emperor, Henry V.

1119	(20 August) Henry defeats Louis VI at the Battle of Brémule.
1120	(25 November) Henry's only legitimate son, William, is drowned in the wreck of the *White Ship*.
1125	The Emperor, Henry V, dies.
1126	The English barons pay homage to Matilda as heiress to the throne of England.
1128	Matilda marries Geoffrey Plantagenet.
1133	Matilda's first son, Henry Plantagenet, is born.
1135	(1 December) King Henry dies. (22 December) His nephew Stephen, Count of Boulogne, is crowned.
1138	Robert, Earl of Gloucester, renounces his allegiance to Stephen. (22 August) David, King of Scots, is defeated at the Battle of the Standard.
1139	The Bishop of Salisbury and his family are arrested. Matilda arrives in England.
1141	(2 February) Stephen is defeated and captured at the Battle of Lincoln. (14 September) Earl Robert is captured at Winchester and (November) is exchanged for Stephen.
1145	Geoffrey Plantagenet completes his conquest of Normandy. King Louis VII of France recognizes him as duke.
1147	Matilda leaves England.
1151	Henry Plantagenet succeeds his father as Count of Anjou and Duke of Normandy.
1153	(6 November) Stephen concludes a treaty with Henry at Winchester and recognizes him as his heir.
1154	(25 October) Stephen dies.

Genealogical tree

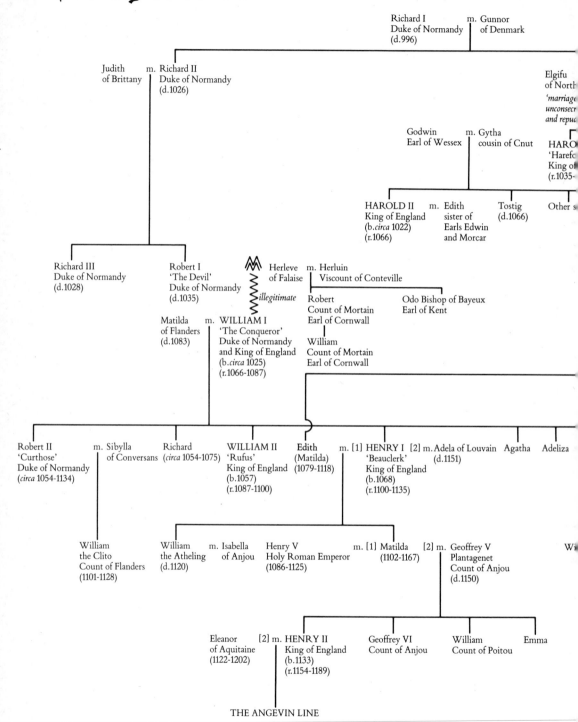

Richard I
Duke of Normandy
(d.996)

m. Gunnor
of Denmark

Judith
of Brittany

m. Richard II
Duke of Normandy
(d.1026)

Elgifu
of North
'marriage
unconsecr
and repuc

Godwin
Earl of Wessex

m. Gytha
cousin of Cnut

HARO
'Harefo
King of
(r.1035-

HAROLD II
King of England
(b.circa 1022)
(r.1066)

m. Edith
sister of
Earls Edwin
and Morcar

Tostig
(d.1066)

Other s

Richard III
Duke of Normandy
(d.1028)

Robert I
'The Devil'
Duke of Normandy
(d.1035)

Herleve
of Falaise

m. Herluin
Viscount of Conteville

illegitimate

Matilda
of Flanders
(d.1083)

m. WILLIAM I
'The Conqueror'
Duke of Normandy
and King of England
(b.circa 1025)
(r.1066-1087)

Robert
Count of Mortain
Earl of Cornwall

Odo Bishop of Bayeux
Earl of Kent

William
Count of Mortain
Earl of Cornwall

Robert II
'Curthose'
Duke of Normandy
(circa 1054-1134)

m. Sibylla
of Conversans

Richard
(circa 1054-1075)

WILLIAM II
'Rufus'
King of England
(b.1057)
(r.1087-1100)

Edith
(Matilda)
(1079-1118)

m. [1] HENRY I [2] m. Adela of Louvain
'Beauclerk'
King of England
(b.1068)
(r.1100-1135)

(d.1151)

Agatha   Adeliza

William
the Clito
Count of Flanders
(1101-1128)

William
the Atheling
(d.1120)

m. Isabella
of Anjou

Henry V
Holy Roman Emperor
(1086-1125)

m. [1] Matilda
(1102-1167)

[2] m. Geoffrey V
Plantagenet
Count of Anjou
(d.1150)

W

Eleanor
of Aquitaine
(1122-1202)

[2] m. HENRY II
King of England
(b.1133)
(r.1154-1189)

Geoffrey VI
Count of Anjou

William
Count of Poitou

Emma

THE ANGEVIN LINE

216

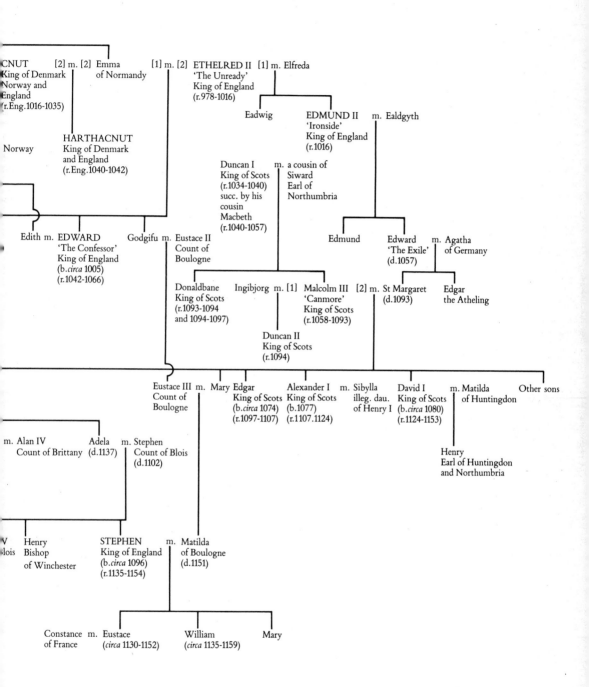

CNUT [2] m. [2] Emma [1] m. [2] ETHELRED II [1] m. Elfreda
King of Denmark of Normandy 'The Unready'
Norway and King of England
England (r.978-1016)
(r.Eng.1016-1035)

Eadwig EDMUND II m. Ealdgyth
'Ironside'
King of England
(r.1016)

Norway HARTHACNUT
King of Denmark
and England
(r.Eng.1040-1042)

Duncan I m. a cousin of
King of Scots Siward
(r.1034-1040) Earl of
succ. by his Northumbria
cousin
Macbeth
(r.1040-1057)

Edith m. EDWARD Godgifu m. Eustace II Edmund Edward m. Agatha
'The Confessor' Count of 'The Exile' of Germany
King of England Boulogne (d.1057)
(b.circa 1005)
(r.1042-1066)

Donaldbane Ingibjorg m. [1] Malcolm III [2] m. St Margaret Edgar
King of Scots 'Canmore' (d.1093) the Atheling
(r.1093-1094 King of Scots
and 1094-1097) (r.1058-1093)

Duncan II
King of Scots
(r.1094)

Eustace III m. Mary Edgar Alexander I m. Sibylla David I m. Matilda Other sons
Count of King of Scots King of Scots illeg. dau. King of Scots of Huntingdon
Boulogne (b.circa 1074) (b.1077) of Henry I (b.circa 1080)
(r.1097-1107) (r.1107.1124) (r.1124-1153)

m. Alan IV Adela m. Stephen Henry
Count of Brittany (d.1137) Count of Blois Earl of Huntingdon
(d.1102) and Northumbria

V Henry STEPHEN m. Matilda
lois Bishop King of England of Boulogne
of Winchester (b.circa 1096) (d.1151)
(r.1135-1154)

Constance m. Eustace William Mary
of France (circa 1130-1152) (circa 1135-1159)

Select bibliography

CONTEMPORARY SOURCES

The Anglo-Saxon Chronicle, trans. G. N. Garmonsway (1953)

The Bayeux Tapestry, ed. Sir Frank Stenton (1957)

Chronicles of the Reigns of Stephen, Henry II and Richard I, ed. R. Howlett (1886)

Chronicon Petroburgense, ed. T. Stapleton (1849)

Eadmer, *Historia Novorum and Vita Sancti Anselmi*, ed. M. Rule (1884), *Historia Novorum* trans. G. Bosanquet (1964).

English Historical Documents 1042–1189, ed. D. C. Douglas and G. W. Greenaway (1953)

Florence of Worchester, *Chronicon ex Chronicis,* ed. B. Thorpe (1849), trans. T. Forester (1854)

Geoffrey Gaimar, *L'estorie des Engles*, ed. A. Bell (1960), ed. and trans. Sir Thomas Hardy and C. T. Martin (1889)

Gerald of Wales, *De Rebus a se Gestis*, ed. and trans. H. E. Butler (1937)

Gervase of Canterbury, *Opera Historica*, ed. W. Stubbs (1879)

Gesta Stephani Regis Anglorum et Ducis Normanorum, ed. and trans. K. R. Potter (1955)

Guy of Amiens, *Carmen de Hastingae Proelio*, ed. and trans. C. Morton and H. Muntz (1972)

Henry of Huntington, *Historia Anglorum*, trans. T. Forester (1853) ed. T. Arnold (1879)

John of Salisbury, *Opera Omnia*, ed. J. A. Giles (1848)

The Laws of the English Kings from Edward to Henry I, ed. A. J. Robertson (1925)

Orderic Vitalis, *Historica Ecclesiastica*, ed. and trans. M. Chibnall (1969–1973)

William of Jumièges, *Gesta Normanorum Ducum*, ed. J. Marx (Rouen and Paris 1914)

William of Malmesbury, *De Gestis Regum Anglorum*, ed. W. Stubbs (1889) *Historia Novella*, ed. and trans, K. R. Potter (1955)

William of Poitiers, *Gesta Guillelmi Ducis Normanorum et Regis Anglorum*, ed. and trans. R. Foreville (Paris 1952)

SECONDARY AUTHORITIES

M. Ashley, *The Life and Times of William I* (1973)
R. Barber, *Henry Plantagenet* (1964)
F. Barlow, *William I and the Norman Conquest* (1965)
  Edward the Confessor (1970)
  The Feudal Kingdom of England 1042–1216 (revised 1972)
G. W. S. Barrow, *Feudal Britain* (1956)
J. Beeler, *Warfare in England 1066–1189* (Cornell, 1966)
C. N. L. Brook, *From Alfred to Henry III* (1961)
  The Saxon and Norman Kings (1963)
Z. N. Brooke, *The English Church and the Papacy from the Conquest to
  the Reign of King John* (1931)
R. A. Brown, *The Normans and the Norman Conquest* (1969)
Lt. Col. A. H. Burne, *The Battlefields of England* (1950)
  More Battlefields of England (1952)
The Cambridge Medieval History, Vol. V (1926)
Sir Alfred Clapham, *English Romanesque Architecture after the
  Conquest* (1934)
J. Clayton, *St. Anselm* (Milwaukee, 1933)
G. G. Coulton, *Life in the Middle Ages* (reprint of 2nd edn. 1954)
H. A. Cronne, *The Reign of Stephen* (1970)
C. W. David, *Robert Curthose, Duke of Normandy* (Cambridge,
  Mass., 1920)
H. W. C. Davis, *England under the Normans and Angevins* (13th edn.
  1949)
R. H. C. Davis, *King Stephen* (1967)
  The Normans and their Myth (1976)
D. C. Douglas, *William the Conqueror* (1964)
  The Norman Achievement (1969)
E. A. Freeman, *The History of the Norman Conquest of England*
  (1867–1879)
  The Reign of William Rufus and the Accession of Henry I (1882)
V. H. Galbraith, *The Making of Domesday Book* (1961)
D. Grinnell-Milne, *The Killing of William Rufus* (1968)
C. H. Haskins, *The Normans in European History* (New York, 1915)
C. W. Hollister, *The Military Organisation of Norman England* (1965)
E. J. Keeley, *Roger of Salisbury* (Berkeley, 1972)
Lt. Col. C. H. Lemmon, *The Field of Hastings* (1956)
Sir John Lloyd, *The History of Wales from the Earliest Times to the
  Edwardian Conquest* (3rd edn. 1939)
H. R. Loyn, *Anglo-Saxon England and the Norman Conquest* (1965)
A. J. MacDonald, *Lanfranc* (1926)
F. W. Maitland, *Domesday Book and Beyond* (1960)

D. J. A. Matthew, *The Norman Conquest* (1966)

Sir Charles Oman, *England Before the Norman Conquest* (9th edn. 1949)

J. Le Patourel, *The Norman Empire* (1976)

A. L. Poole, *From Domesday Book to Magna Carta* (2nd edn. 1955)

J. Enoch Powell and K. Wallis, *The House of Lords in the Middle Ages* (1968)

D. F. Renn, *Norman Castles in Britain* (1968)

R. L. G. Ritchie, *The Normans and Scotland* (1954)

O. Rössler, *Kaiserin Mathilde* (Berlin, 1897)

J. H. Round, *Feudal England* (1909)
  Geoffrey de Mandeville: a Study in Anarchy (1892)

A.Saltman, *Theobald, Arıhbishop of Canterbury* (1956)

D. M. Stenton, *English Society in the Early Middle Ages* (1951)
  English Justice 1066–1215 (Philadelphia, 1964)

Sir Frank Stenton, *Anglo-Saxon England* (2nd edn. 1947)
  The First Century of English Feudalism 1066–1166 (2nd. edn. 1961)
  William the Conqueror (2nd Edn. 1967)

W. R. W. Stephens, *The English Church 1066–1272* (1901)

L. Voss, *Heinrich von Blois* (Berlin, 1932)

P. Zumthor, *Guillaume le Conquérant* (Paris 1964)

Index